Asian Americans in Transition

Stanley Karnow
Nancy Yoshihara

Foreword by
Senator Daniel K. Inouye

The Asia Society is a nonprofit educational organization dedicated to increasing American understanding of the culture, history and contemporary affairs of the more than thirty countries broadly defined as the Asia-Pacific region.

This publication was made possible by generous funding from the Freedom Forum, through the courtesy of Bette Bao Lord.

Design by David Harvey and Timothy Horn.

Published in 1992 in the United States of America
by The Asia Society, 725 Park Avenue, New York, NY 10021

ISBN 0-878-48-506-6

Printed and bound in the United States of America

Contents

Foreword

In October 1991 The Asia Society hosted a national conference in Los Angeles on Asian Americans. Over a period of three days, distinguished Asian American and other panelists examined issues facing Americans of Asian ancestry in the final decade of the 20th century. By coincidence, the conference was held shortly after the U.S. Census Bureau had published its 1990 population figures. These figures revealed a significant shift in the demographics of the American social landscape, especially in states like California, Texas, New York and Illinois, where the population of minority groups showed major gains. Asian Americans have almost doubled their numbers in each of the past three decades, making them the fastest growing segment of the U.S. population. The impact of the increase was touched upon at The Asia Society's conference, but determining its real significance will require extensive analysis by researchers over the next several years.

Composed of no fewer than 20 different ethnic subgroups, the Asian American community is one of the most diverse and complex minority groups in the nation, and thus difficult to define. The group includes Americans of the fourth, fifth and even sixth generations as well as first-generation immigrants and refugees. While these groups share some cultural traditions, the differences between them are frequently more pronounced than the similarities. There is no common language among them. The more recently arrived often feel estranged from other Asian groups, especially those with whom they have strong historical differences.

More often than not, mainstream America lumps Asian Americans into one group, ignoring the sometimes wide differences among the various ethnic communities. As a whole, Asian Americans are perceived by the mainstream as hardworking achievers who are willing to accept their lot without complaining, a model against which other ethnic minority groups are measured. The image of Asian Americans as a model for other minorities not only does damage to relations between Asian Americans and their Latino and African American brothers and sisters, but it has an equally devastating effect on many Asian Americans themselves. While many among the more established and assimilated groups have achieved a relative degree of success, a large number of Asian Americans live at poverty levels, are poorly educated, and are ignored in social assistance programs. Asian Americans, it is believed, either do not need assistance or will be taken care of by members of their own communities. The Asian American underclasses, found primarily among the refugees and recent immigrants, are victims of the "model minority" myth, as are those Asian Americans who are more successful but limited in their potential because of cultural misperceptions that result from racial stereotyping and prejudice.

Asian Americans have endured much in the approximately 150 years they have been in the United States: the Chinese, the first Asians to settle in this country, were consigned to labor gangs to help build the Transcontinental–Central Pacific Railroad in the 1860s; more than 100,000 Japanese Americans were forced to relocate to internment camps during World War II; and the Vietnamese "boat people," driven here after war ravaged their country, struggled to adjust to the unfamiliar conditions of a new homeland. But as Asian immigrants strove to make a better life for themselves here, they also helped to transform and enrich their adopted country. As the nation grew during the past 150 years, Asians could be found contributing to all sectors of the economy, including the sugar and pineapple plantations of Hawaii, the farms and orchards of California, the lumber towns of Washington and the many small businesses and factories of major American cities.

Asians have made much progress in the relatively short period they have been in the United States. But in recent times, they have become scapegoats in a nation grown tense over relations with Japan, and over relations among its own racial groups. The trade imbalance with Japan, exacerbated by the regrettable statements of Japanese government leaders critical of American workers and the subsequent and short-sighted "Buy American" campaign at home, is triggering a backlash against Asian Americans. We have seen all this happen before, with tragic consequences.

Many recall in vivid and horrible detail the 1982 beating death of Vincent Chin in Detroit, a city wracked by the upheaval in the automobile industry. Chin was bludgeoned to death with baseball bats by assailants who mistook him for a Japanese. And in the aftermath of the April 1992 verdict in the Rodney King beating case, Asian American–owned businesses became targets for looting and destruction in Los Angeles. All of this came about just after the U.S. Civil Rights Commission had announced its findings that "Asian Americans face widespread prejudice, discrimination and denials of equal opportunity. In addition, many Asian Americans, particularly those who are immigrants, are deprived of equal access to public services, including police protection, education, health care and the judicial system."

In the face of this, it would seem that racism and its attendant problems are so formidable and overwhelming that we do not even know how to begin to deal with the crisis. But we must do so if we are to emerge from the ashes of the Los Angeles debacle and from the smoldering racial tensions in communities across the country. We have made much progress since the nation last grappled with the worst effects of racial hatred in the 1960s. But as the aftermath of the Rodney King verdict showed us again, we Americans need to progress where it really counts—in the hearts and spirits of our people.

As we enter the 21st century, we are on the threshold of a changing America that will, for the first time in our nation's history, see the "minorities" begin to constitute a major segment of our nation's people. Asian Americans, in the midst of these changes, can play a significant and lasting role. Our collective memories hold the not-too-distant struggles of our immigrant grandparents and parents, echoed in the experiences of more recent arrivals to our shores, and we recognize that we are the beneficiaries of those earlier immigrants who struggled silently against seemingly impossible odds to gain their place in America. Like those who came before us, we have an opportunity to enrich the definition of who and what Americans are.

In many respects the Asian American experience parallels that of other Americans, most of whom are themselves descended from immigrants. This thoughtful and informed account by Stanley Karnow and Nancy Yoshihara, in illuminating the Asian American experience, will enlarge the understanding of us all.

Senator Daniel K. Inouye
May 1992

Preface

This report by Stanley Karnow and Nancy Yoshihara had its origins in an effort by The Asia Society to broaden awareness of the growing Asian American community and its roles and concerns. As America's leading organization dedicated to strengthening understanding of Asia and communication between Asians and Americans, the Society has long believed that Asian Americans are both a force linking this country to Asia and a resource for educating all Americans about Asia. In order for Asian Americans to contribute fully to U.S.-Asia understanding, however, it is essential that their history, make-up, achievements and problems be more widely appreciated in our society.

To this end, The Asia Society and 23 Asian American organizations co-sponsored a national symposium in Los Angeles on October 24–26, 1991, on the theme "The Asian American Experience: Looking Ahead." Attended by more than 900 people, the symposium examined issues of Asian American involvement in culture and values, education, work, the arts, communities and politics, with an emphasis on future needs and tasks. To the best of the Society's knowledge, this was the first such effort to have representatives of diverse Asian American groups from around the country focus on shared concerns.

In preparing for the symposium the Society realized that there were few if any comprehensive yet succinct published descriptions of the Asian American population and the challenges it faces. We concluded that the symposium could help fill this gap and asked Stanley Karnow and Nancy Yoshihara if they would draw on the symposium discussions as well as their own knowledge, and other research, to prepare this booklet. We agreed that our goal was to produce a "high-quality primer" on the Asian American experience which would help politicians and government officials, business people and journalists, educators and students, social service providers and foundation executives to understand and deal more effectively with Asian Americans and their concerns.

The Asia Society is very gratified by the result and wishes to thank Mr. Karnow and Ms. Yoshihara for the skill, discipline and dedication they brought to the task. We are fortunate indeed that two such able and busy people were willing to devote themselves to this project. While the report was being written, riots broke out in Los Angeles and other American cities; one clear implication of those events and their tragic impact on Asian Americans is that public education about Asian Americans is sorely needed. The authors and the Society hope this report will help fill that need.

The Asia Society also wishes to thank a number of individuals and organizations whose support for the larger project helped make this publication possible. Bharati Mukherjee, Michael Woo, Richard Sherwood and David Murdock chaired the symposium organizing committee. John Y. Tateishi and Faranak Van Patten deserve great credit for planning and masterfully orchestrating the symposium. We are particularly grateful to the Asian American and other participants in the symposium whose insights are reflected in this report. Financial support for the project as a whole came from a number of sources listed elsewhere in these pages. The editing and production of this report were very ably handled by Deborah Field Washburn and Sayu Bhojwani of the Society's staff, and its publication has been aided by a generous grant from the Freedom Forum through the good offices of Bette Bao Lord.

Marshall M. Bouton
Executive Vice President
The Asia Society
May 1992

Asian
Americans in
Transition

1

Introduction

Asian Americans are the fastest growing segment of the U.S. population. During the past 20 years, their ranks have more than tripled to 7.3 million, or nearly 3 percent of the population. Even more dramatic has been their thirtyfold increase since 1940, when they totaled fewer than 250,000. By the end of the century, they will probably reach some 10 million.

This phenomenal growth chiefly owes its impetus to an immigration law enacted in 1965, which abolished the racial quotas that until then had given overwhelming preference to Europeans. President Lyndon B. Johnson, signing the law at the Statue of Liberty, vowed that it would repair "a deep and painful flaw in the fabric of American justice." But nobody foresaw its eventual impact. Robert Kennedy, who as the attorney general during his brother's administration had favored the legislation, estimated that though 5,000 Asians might immigrate during the first year, there would not be "any great influx after that." During the 1980s, however, about 2.6 million Asians entered the United States, more than 40 percent of all legal immigrants—roughly equal to the arrivals from Latin America. As a result, with the exception of Japanese Americans, most Americans of Asian descent are foreign-born.

Asian Americans have long comprised the majority of Hawaii's population, and their numbers have risen during the past decade in California and New York, where they have been heavily concentrated for a century and a half. Many of the immigrants among them, feeling insecure in a new and strange land, cluster in Chinatowns, Little Saigons and other such enclaves, where, for one reason or another, some remain for years. But they disperse to other areas faster than other immigrants, so that their presence, though still small, has grown sharply in relation to population in

Asian-American geography

Percentage of all Asian-Americans living in California   40%

Percentage of all Asian-Americans living in metropolitan areas   94%

Top 10 Asian-American metropolitan areas

Los Angeles-Long Beach	955,000
New York City	556,000
Honolulu	526,000
San Francisco	330,000
Oakland	270,000
San Jose	261,000
Anaheim-Santa Ana	249,000
Chicago	230,000
Washington, D.C.	202,000
San Diego	198,000

Source: U.S. Bureau of the Census. 1990 data.

Region of residence

Total U.S. population   Asian-Americans

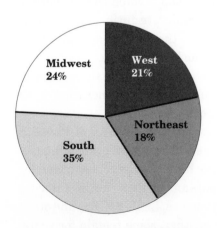

Total U.S. population:
Midwest 24%
West 21%
Northeast 18%
South 35%

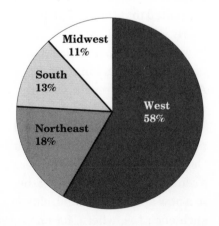

Asian-Americans:
Midwest 11%
South 13%
West 58%
Northeast 18%

Source: U.S. Bureau of the Census. 1990 data.

regions where they were once scarce. Between 1980 and 1990, it more than doubled in Georgia, New Hampshire and Rhode Island, and nearly doubled in Massachusetts, New Jersey, Florida and Wisconsin. Asian Americans currently equal or surpass Hispanics in 12 states and black Americans in 13. It is no longer unusual to discover a Japanese sushi bar or a Vietnamese noodle shop in Des Moines or New Orleans, much less Chinese engineers, Korean grocers and Filipino doctors in Minneapolis or Memphis.

Just as extraordinary is the speed with which newcomers leave urban ghettos for the suburbs. Their moves reflect the elimination of racial housing barriers and a quest for better schools for their children. Their incomes naturally dictate their choice of location. Around New York, the rich have settled in posh places like Westchester and Scarsdale, while the less affluent select areas of Brooklyn and the Bronx. Flushing, in the borough of Queens, is home to so many Asians that one of its subway lines has been dubbed the "Orient Express." In California's Bay Area, the few who can afford it live in such tony spots as Hillsborough and Palo Alto. Monterey Park in Los Angeles County, the only town in the continental United States with an Asian American majority, is mostly composed of upper-middle-class immigrants from Taiwan and Hong Kong, lured there by a Chinese American developer who touted it as an Asian Beverly Hills.

The emergence of Asian Americans has contributed to the nation's evolving demographic profile. The original English colonists created an Anglo-Saxon Protestant portrait of America—an image that later Euro-pean immigrants, despite their differences, were able as whites to fit. But a new pattern unfolded after 1965, when the liberal immigration statute opened the country to Asians and Latin Americans. Combined with African Americans, they have shrunk the white majority in several areas. Los Angeles, for instance, has become a kaleidoscope of minorities—41 percent white, 38 percent Hispanic, 10 percent black and 10 percent Asian American. And other cities are going through a similar evolution.

This trend augurs a period of cultural, racial and ethnic multiplicity that could alter America's values, tastes and even national psyche—and, in the process, reshape its political, economic and social structures.

From its founding, as George Washington envisioned it, the United States would fuse "the oppressed and persecuted of all Nations and Religions [into] *one people.*" Immigrants were exhorted to renounce their past and merge in a "melting pot." Applied only to white Europeans, the theory at first seemed to be working as millions, while preserving many of their native traits, embraced the American creed, but Washington's vision was not universally accepted. Xenophobic movements periodically arose to condemn the intrusion of "foreigners" while foes of assimilation, like the Jewish American philosopher Horace Kallen, refused to be "dissolved in the crucible." What ultimately eroded the concept, however, were not these objections but, as Nathan Glazer and Daniel P. Moynihan maintain in *Beyond the Melting Pot*, the "disinclination of the third and fourth generation of newcomers to blend into a standard, uniform national type." Hence, they observe, the notion of "an intense and unprecedented mixture of ethnic and religious groups in American life . . . has outlived its usefulness, and also its credibility."

Despite the effectiveness of civil rights legislation, the economic and social conditions of black Americans as a whole have deteriorated since the 1960s. For this and other reasons, black militants have called for racial separatism, inspiring many other nonwhite Americans, along with gay and female activists, to profess their identities as a way of asserting themselves. They have been decried by critics who portend a society split by factionalism, rife with tension, difficult to govern. The controversy has sparked a battle, particularly on campuses, over "multiculturalism," as the issue is labeled, and it has been exaggerated by ideologues on both sides as well as by the press. But in many respects the dispute mirrors real concerns over the balance between *pluribus* and *unum* as the United States strives to redefine itself. Whatever its outcome, the idyllic Norman Rockwell picture of America appears to be obsolete.

The vision of a peacefully pluralistic United States sustained a particularly severe blow in Los Angeles in April 1992, when black and Hispanic rioters attacked Korean American merchants following the acquittal of the four policemen in the Rodney King case. The violence, while widely depicted as racial, also reflected deeply rooted economic differences that largely stemmed from the resentment of poor blacks and Hispanics against Korean immigrants who have achieved a measure of success as shopkeepers. So the idea that "people of color" are unified appears to have been subverted, in part at least, by class distinctions.

Some Asian Americans, especially in academic circles, denounce "Anglo conformity," as Professor Sucheng Chan of the University of California at Santa Barbara terms it. She favors a "two-tiered kind of ethnic identity" under which Americans would retain their heritage while interacting with each other. "What peoples of color ask," she has said, "is that we enlarge the sense of inclusiveness so that those who are not of European background can feel finally that they have a stake in American society." Bharati Mukherjee, a writer of Indian descent, offers a different nuance. While supporting pluralism, she cautions that "fracturing the national identity" could poison race relations. "I am against policies that artificially encourage disparateness," she has said. "I want to avoid as much as possible cultural Balkanization."

Asian Americans are themselves multicultural. Tracing their origins back to China, Japan, Korea, the Philippines, Vietnam, Cambodia, Laos, Thailand, Indonesia, Malaysia, India, Pakistan, Bangladesh and different regions in those countries, they include both newcomers and those whose families have long been in the United States. So their diversity defies generalizations. As Professor Roger Daniels of the University of Cincinnati has noted, "The conglomerate image of Asian Americans is a chimera." There may be a certain historical validity in treating them as a "minority," but they are in reality "very distinct minorities." Thus to portray them as cohesive is as misleading as to equate Swedish with Serbian Americans because both are of European extraction. They are further divided by class and by the fact that the majority are newcomers who often have little in common with those whose families have been in the United States for generations.

Some Asian Americans, lamenting the estrangement of others from their heritage, dub them "bananas," or "yellow on the outside and white on the inside," and the jibe is not entirely inaccurate. Very few second or third generation Asian Americans speak the language of their forebears, and even their ethnic organizations conduct their meetings in English. Increasing numbers, particularly among those of Japanese and Chinese descent, are marrying white Americans. Like Jewish or Italian Americans, many evoke their past only by indulging in traditional food. They resemble most other Americans, for whom the culture of their ancestors has virtually faded away.

Ironically, though, the children of Asian Americans deeply rooted in the United States have been in the vanguard of the movement to proclaim their identity by establishing ethnic studies centers and advocacy groups. In that regard they conform to the formulation of Marcus Lee Hansen, the great pioneer in immigration history: "What the son wishes to forget the grandson wishes to remember." But they differ from newcomers, many of whom prefer to remain silent, either because they are too

5

preoccupied with gaining a foothold in America or feel that they are still "guests" in their adopted land.

Asian Americans sometimes derogate green immigrants as "FOBs"— "fresh off the boat." But the newcomers are not easy to classify. A mosaic of peoples whose languages, customs, foods and religions differ, they rarely mix despite efforts by advocacy groups to unite them, and they are also marked by class, regional and political differences. The South Vietnamese officials and entrepreneurs who escaped to America to flee communism bear little resemblance to the peasants who arrived later. Indian Americans advertising for spouses invariably specify caste and provincial origin. In 1990 a New York parade to promote ethnic solidarity broke up when Taiwanese Americans, demanding independence for Taiwan, were assailed by Chinese Americans insisting that the island belongs to China.

Chinese from the interior of Sichuan or Hmong from the mountains of Laos may be stunned by their first sight of America, but most immigrants are attuned to the United States before they arrive. Many are familiar with American pop culture from American television shows and radio programs, which are broadcast around the world. The Japanese are infatuated with American logos, and Little Leaguers from Taiwan regularly win international baseball titles. Western manners and mores have also penetrated Asia, so that newcomers to the United States frequently land already influenced by the best and the worst of America.

But despite their dissimilarities, Asian Americans share common characteristics. Whether their backgrounds are Confucian, Buddhist, Hindu, Muslim, Christian or animist, they tend to adhere to the concept of filial piety, and see achievement as a way to honor their families. Hence their devotion to classic American virtues—hard work, discipline and a willingness to defer instant fulfillment for the sake of future goals. Above all, they make enormous sacrifices to educate their children—a commitment that reflects their esteem for scholarship, supposedly assures success and also raises their own social status.

By national standards, the aggregate accomplishments of Asian Americans are spectacular. They have the highest median household income, the highest percentage of college graduates, the highest percentage of technological and scientific positions, the highest percentage of professional and managerial jobs, the lowest divorce rate, the lowest unemployment rate, the lowest crime rate. By learning English and naturalizing quickly, newcomers among them adapt to the United States faster than most other immigrants. On the average, they become citizens seven years after their arrival, compared to nine years for South Americans.

The catalog of Asian American celebrities includes five Nobel laureate scientists as well as computer pioneers, artists, actors, musicians, writers, architects, athletes, television personalities and financial wizards. Forever seeking to enshrine the American dream, the news media constantly extol Asian Americans as Horatio Alger heroes. Professor William Petersen, a sociologist at Berkeley, called them the "model minority"—a term, wrote Louis Winnick in *Commentary* recently, that is yesterday's coinage: "By now, Asian Americans have vaulted to a more exalted station—America's trophy population."

Asian American advocacy groups deplore such adulation, arguing that to spotlight successful Asian Americans blurs the difficulties that face many of those who are struggling to survive. The complaint is largely justified.

If the median incomes of Chinese, Japanese, Korean, Filipino and Indian American households match or surpass the national average, those of Vietnamese, Cambodian and Laotian refugees lag behind. The bottom of the ladder is apparent in big-city Chinatowns, where newcomers live in tenements and work as peddlers, waiters and dishwashers. Conditions are especially grim for garment workers, most of them women, who are often paid below- minimum wages. While many early Southeast Asian refugees have thrived, many later arrivals languish on welfare. Numbers of teenagers are school valedictorians, yet many drop out because they cannot adjust to America. Adapting to a new land also strains immigrant families. There are increasing instances of divorce, children breaking away from parents and the elderly being neglected. According to social workers, such cases are underreported because of a propensity among Asians to hide their personal problems from strangers.

A recent study by the U.S. Civil Rights Commission concluded that Asian Americans are not spared racial prejudice. Many are blocked from rising into corporate board rooms by a "glass ceiling"—a hurdle they often overcome by starting their own companies. Though Asian Americans are breaking records in education, some colleges allegedly curb their admissions through disguised quotas.

Asian Americans are also nagged by racial harassment and even violence. Black Americans in Brooklyn and Los Angeles have boycotted Korean grocers, and some incidents have resulted in killings. In 1987 white youths beat an Indian American to death in Jersey City, and two years later young whites killed a Chinese immigrant in North Carolina. But most attention has revolved around the murder in Detroit in 1982 of Vincent Chin, a Chinese American, by two jobless automobile workers who reportedly mistook him for a Japanese and blamed him for their plight. The case confirmed what Asian Americans have long known: despite their diversity, they all look alike to other Americans.

A recent phenomenon has been the growth of Asian criminal groups that chiefly prey on Asian Americans. The large Vietnamese refugee community in California is plagued by Vietnamese gangs that torture and rob their victims in their homes. An even more serious menace are Chinese syndicates, linked to Hong Kong and Taiwan groups, which are involved in prostitution, extortion, illegal gambling, heroin trafficking and the exploitation of immigrants, especially in the Chinatowns of New York and San Francisco. Many of their crimes are politically motivated. Vietnamese extremists have killed Vietnamese whom they suspected of being pro-Communist. In 1984 a Taiwan group murdered Henry Liu, a Chinese American journalist who had criticized the Nationalist regime.

What lies ahead for Asian Americans is a matter of conjecture. Intermarriage with whites, a growing trend, may dilute their identity. Though divorce among them is still rare, couples are increasingly separating as numbers of immigrant Asian American women, like other American women, strive for emancipation and equality. Families face further pressure as their children, like other American children, defy parental authority. Surveys of Asian American students show that, by the third or fourth generation, they perform no better than white youngsters. On the other hand, Asian Americans may retain many of their traits in a pluralistic future, in which case the United States will benefit—as it has from every ethnic infusion in its history.

Over the years, Asian Americans have overcome daunting barriers to gain their place in American society—which, far too often, treated them shabbily. To borrow sociologist Peter Rose's phrase, if they are regarded today as paragons, they were viewed only yesterday as pariahs.

2

History

Few chapters in the nation's history are as disgraceful as the mistreatment of the Asians who came to America. For nearly a century they were subjected to both popular and institutional harassment, and some even died at the hands of lynch mobs. But they showed extraordinary fortitude in the face of overwhelming odds, and their perseverance stands as testimony to their commitment to the United States.

The discovery of gold in 1848 lured prospectors to California from around the world. Thousands were Chinese, but they were not the first Asians to set foot in America. Prehistoric Asian nomads crossed the land bridge that is now the Bering Strait to become American Indians. Myth has it that Chinese monks explored America centuries later. From the 17th century on, Chinese and Filipinos were living in Mexico, having arrived by galleon from Manila, and some drifted into Louisiana, then a Spanish territory. By the late 1700s, Asian crewmen on a clipper ship back from China had gone ashore in Baltimore, and a Pennsylvania squire had Chinese servants. A few Chinese merchants, probably former employees of American trading firms based in Canton, settled in San Francisco. Chinese officials had long lumped Americans together with other Westerners as "barbarians" only out for profit. But soon they realized that America was a separate nation whose industrial achievements might serve China.

Nor did Americans know much about Asia. Japan was *terra incognita*. Like many European intellectuals, Benjamin Franklin fancied China to be a model society. Numbers of American entrepreneurs subsequently saw China as a market for American exports, and they further welcomed Chinese to the United States as cheap labor. Some American missionaries patronized the Chinese as potential Christians while others, frustrated by their failure to convert them, decried their "pagan" ways. As they did the arrival of other immigrants, nativists opposed the influx of Chinese and other immigrants into America, and white workers, fearing competition, were equally antagonistic. American opinion seesawed as social, economic and political conditions changed. But, by the late 19th century, it was almost universally hostile toward the Chinese newcomers.

Some 300,000 Chinese poured into the United States during the 19th century. Another 50,000 went to Hawaii, then an independent kingdom, to work on American-owned plantations. Like many Europeans, most were sojourners who returned home. Those who remained spent their lives working to support the families they had left behind. The single men seldom married, since laws barred them from marrying white women and the few Chinese women brought to America were chiefly prostitutes. Thus, until after World War II, the Chinese in America were mostly bachelors—a phenomenon visible today in the scarcity of those whose lineage goes back more than three generations.

By 1852 more than 20,000 Chinese had fled the rebellions and natural calamities roiling China to seek gold in *Gam Saan*, o "Gold Mountain," the Cantonese term for California. Most came under the auspices of Chinese labor contractors, borrowing to pay their passage. At first greeted warmly, they were invited to march in a funeral procession for President Zachary Taylor in 1850, and to attend a celebration marking California's admission to the Union later that year. A "worthy integer of our population," the *Alta California* called them in 1852: "The China boys will yet vote at the same polls, study at the same schools and bow at the same altar as our countrymen."

As the gold ran out, some 10,000 Chinese joined the gangs building the intercontinental railroad, carving out the route over the Sierra Nevada mountains—a feat that cost them more than 1,000 lives but gained them little gratitude. They also turned to fishing, farming and land reclamation, and spurred California's dramatic economic growth. Many settled in San Francisco and other cities to make shoes, cigars and clothing, or run laundries and restaurants, and they became coveted domestic servants. Some spread into Georgia and Mississippi as agricultural workers.

Their thrift and hard work were undoubted, yet it was precisely for that reason that they alarmed white labor. Or as a Chinese writer put it at the time, they were persecuted "not for their vices, but for their virtues."

Though Americans preached assimilation, the assumption was

repeatedly tested as European newcomers aroused the ire of chauvinists. During most of the 19th century, however, the federal government refused to curb immigration, which provided the manpower needed to develop its vast resources. But in California and the other western states, anti-Chinese sentiment rose to a pitch of hysteria that foreshadowed resistance throughout the country to all immigrants. Hence the fate of the Chinese augured a national trend.

No sooner did they reach California than they faced discriminatory laws and ordinances. One was a miners' tax imposed on aliens ineligible for naturalization—which under a federal law of 1790 was limited to "free white persons." In 1852 Governor John Bigler proposed a halt to Chinese immigration into the state. Two years later, a statute that prohibited blacks and Indians from testifying against whites was construed by the state supreme court to include Chinese. The decision not only deprived them of legal protection, but in effect entitled whites to assault them with impunity.

The city of San Francisco, equally tough, ruled that tenements must provide 500 cubic feet of air for each inhabitant, but the ordinance was enforced only in Chinatown. Resistance meant jail, where the Chinese were required to have their traditional queues cut off. Chinese laundries were forced to pay exorbitant licensing fees. A regulation banned shoulder poles, a common Chinese device, and another proscribed firecrackers, a Chinese invention.

California's mercantile and financial interests were generally sympathetic toward the Chinese, mainly out of fear that restricting them would imperil trade with China. Big capitalists, eager to exploit their labor, also welcomed them. In a state that largely opposed slavery before the Civil War, however, many viewed them as slaves in disguise. Others, appalled by China's reputed despotism and depravity, could not conceive of them as ideal Americans. Wearing floppy clothes, basket hats and braided queues, and speaking a baffling tongue, they were seen as distinct—a perception confirmed by lurid accounts of Chinatowns as enclaves of prostitutes and opium addicts. They were easy prey for roughnecks, who, in the wild frontier spirit of the era, constantly abused foreigners. Their family and regional associations, though not unlike those of other immigrants, aroused suspicion that they owed their loyalties to sinister organizations. These attitudes fit theories of white superiority then widely believed in America. Above all, the Chinese were convenient scapegoats for various economic and political groups.

Contrary to the conventional view of them as passive, the Chinese fought back in the courts, and all the local ordinances against them were ultimately voided. The Chinese Benevolent Association, known as the Chinese Six Companies because it comprised diverse regional groups, hired white lawyers, who carried some of the cases up to the U.S. Supreme Court. They were helped by the Fourteenth Amendment and the Civil Rights Act of 1870, which guaranteed them equality. California's bid to block Chinese immigration, for example, was annulled on the grounds that immigration was a federal matter. In many instances, judges who detested the Chinese nevertheless ruled for them out of respect for the law.

But white juries often disregarded their right to testify. Nor could the courts stop whites from attacking them. The worst riot erupted in 1885 in Rock Springs, Wyoming, where white miners killed 28 Chinese. The brutality was partly inspired by the rise in California of the Workingmen's Party, largely composed of jobless white workers hit by the recession that followed the Civil War. Blaming the Chinese for their plight, they rallied behind Denis Kearny, a fiery Irish immigrant whose slogan was: "The Chinese Must Go!" Successful in the state elections held in 1878, the movement was soon a force in California politics.

Mark Twain defended the Chinese, as did Senator Charles Sumner of Massachusetts. With its abolitionist tradition, New England was especially compassionate. Several Chinese students attended Yale, where they were lodged by local families. A few became college baseball and football stars, and a young Chinese coxed the crew that defeated Harvard in 1880 and 1881.

Organized labor promoted the crusade against the Chinese as racism eclipsed class consciousness. The economist Henry George, a foremost critic of capitalism, called for their expulsion. They were condemned by Samuel Gompers, founder of the American Federation of Labor, and by Jack London, who said, "I am first of all a white man and only then a Socialist." Bret Harte had meant to be ironic, but his immensely popular poem, published in 1870, engraved on American minds an indelible image of the devious Chinese:

> That for ways that are dark
> And tricks that are vain,
> The heathen Chinee is peculiar. . . .

The Chinese issue took on wider dimensions during the early 1870s, as both Democrats and Republicans bid for the support of California, where the margin between the two parties was slim and a tilt could swing a national election. The Democrats had the edge, having backed white labor, while the Republicans were bedeviled by a treaty signed by their administration in 1868, which pledged free Chinese immigration in exchange for American trade privileges in China. Named for Anson Burlingame, a former American diplomat who had represented China, the treaty had been swiftly ratified by the Republican majority in the Senate.

In 1880 the Republicans sponsored a new treaty that would "regulate, limit or suspend" the immigration of Chinese laborers. The next measures followed inexorably. In 1882 Congress enacted a law that "suspended" the entry of Chinese laborers for ten years, and further laws barred them permanently. These were the only immigration laws in American history aimed at a specific nationality.

Though some 300,000 Chinese came to the United States during the 19th century, more than half of them returned home. The exclusion acts further thinned their ranks, so that by 1940 they numbered fewer than 60,000. Some merchants flourished, and exemptions under the law permitted them to bring in wives and raise families. But most Chinese were poor bachelors relegated to Chinatowns, where they worked in restaurants and at other menial jobs. The Chinese laundryman who labored around the clock and slept in his shop personified their solitude.

Officials arbitrarily raided Chinatowns and deported anyone unable to show a residence certificate. New arrivals were often detained for months on Angel Island, a transient center in San Francisco Bay. Denied naturalization, they lacked the political influence to plead their cause. Nor could they count on the weak regime in China to intervene on their behalf, as the Japanese government did, with uneven results, for its compatriots in the United States.

The Japanese experience in America both resembled and differed from that of the Chinese. Long prohibited from traveling abroad by their government, Japanese first went to Hawaii as plantation workers late in the 19th century. They became the largest racial bloc there, and many later crossed to the United States in hopes of improving their lot.

Japan's defeat of Russia in 1905 impressed President Theodore Roosevelt, who sought to protect Japanese Americans from persecution. He discouraged San Francisco officials from segregating their schoolchildren. Despite lobbying by the western states, he also blocked a bill to exclude the Japanese. Instead the United States and Japan reached a compromise on the issue of Japanese immigration in the "Gentleman's Agreement" of 1908, one of whose provisions allowed Japanese women into America. The Japanese in the United States were thus able to sire families, which lent stability and continuity to their community.

But Japanese newcomers, like the Chinese, were denied naturalization. California and other western states also passed laws preventing them from owning land. Yet they persisted and succeeded during the early 20th century. While the Chinese preferred cities, the Japanese spread into rural areas. They leased farms to dodge the land laws—or put the property in the names of their American-born children. Their success was remarkable. Besides producing a major share of California's fruits and vegetables, they dominated the market in many areas through their distribution networks.

Japanese American students excelled. In 1933 the Los Angeles public schools cited only one out of 10,000 for truancy. Of the nine high school valedictorians in Seattle in 1937, three were Nisei, or second generation Japanese Americans. But many college graduates, blocked by racial barriers from professional jobs, could only work on family farms or at fruit stands.

Other Asians were less numerous and less visible than the Chinese and Japanese during the late 19th and early 20th centuries. A few Indians, mostly Punjabi farmers, arrived in California in hopes of earning enough money to return home rich, and their numbers might have increased had not Congress curbed immigration from India and the rest of Asia in 1913. At about the same time, a trickle of Koreans began to reach America. Many were Christians fleeing Japan's rule in Korea. They included Syngman Rhee, who earned a graduate degree at Princeton and became Korea's president when the nation won independence after World War II.

Following America's acquisition of the Philippines in 1899, Filipinos could enter the United States freely, and some 30,000 had arrived by 1930. An early group consisted of students, many of whom returned home to become prominent figures. Later ones, who chiefly came in search of work, spread around the country, mostly performing menial jobs. Many, hired as farm hands, were attacked by employers for staging strikes and by labor unions for displacing white workers, and several died in riots in California. Their immigration was sharply curbed in 1935, when the

Philippine Commonwealth was created as a step toward independence.

Reflecting the nation's insular mood after World War I, Congress virtually halted immigration in 1924 by setting quotas based on national origin—a system that favored Europeans. Not only did the law bar Asians on that basis, but it doubly discriminated against them by excluding groups ineligible for naturalization.

In 1943 President Franklin D. Roosevelt rewarded China, then America's ally in the war against Japan, by persuading Congress to repeal the acts excluding Chinese and denying them naturalization. Even so, the law limited their immigration to only a token. Animosity toward Filipino Americans also abated as Americans learned of the resistance of Filipino troops in the Philippines against the Japanese invasion. But Americans of Japanese origin, aliens and citizens alike, faced a harrowing ordeal soon after Japan's raid on Pearl Harbor on December 7, 1941.

More than 100,000 Japanese Americans were shunted into ten isolated camps reaching from California to Arkansas. Their internment was an unprecedented and ignoble episode based solely on race, since no comparable measure was applied to Americans of German or Italian descent.

Many military intelligence agents as well as J. Edgar Hoover, director of the Federal Bureau of Investigation, dismissed the notion that Japanese Americans were a threat. But senior army officers, politicians, labor unions and others demanded action. Walter Lippmann, the influential press pundit, called the West coast "a combat zone" in which the rights of citizens could be abridged.

The internment order, signed by President Roosevelt on February 19, 1942, was urged on him by Henry L. Stimson, the secretary of war, and Stimson's assistant, John J. McCloy. Models of rectitude, both men knew that relocating citizens on strictly racial grounds was constitutionally dubious. But, like many of their generation, they were prejudiced against people of a different color.

The idea that Japanese Americans could be surrogates for Japan was patently absurd. Of the 3,000 young Japanese Americans tested as potential interpreters, few spoke fluent Japanese. Fighting in Europe, a regiment of Japanese Americans, determined to prove their patriotism, was one of the most decorated units in U.S. history— at a cost of some 9,000 casualties. Daniel Inouye, now a senator from Hawaii, lost his right arm in Italy while serving with that unit.

The Supreme Court upheld the internment decision in three cases, Justice Hugo Black writing the majority opinion in one. Two decades later, though then a strong civil rights advocate, he said, "I would do precisely the same thing today. We had a situation where we were at war."

In 1976, after years of lobbying by Japanese Americans and others, President Gerald Ford formally apologized to the internees, and Congress later voted to indemnify them. The former camp inmates, most of them aged, eventually received $20,000 each. In December 1991, speaking at Pearl Harbor on the 50th anniversary of Japan's attack, President George Bush called them "innocent victims who committed no offense." But a 1991 survey found that 30 percent of Californians viewed the incarceration as justified—an attitude that has left many Japanese Americans feeling hostage to future ties between the United States and Japan.

Asian Americans benefited as racial barriers fell after World War II. California repealed the alien land laws. In 1954 the Supreme Court ended school segregation in its *Brown v. Board of Education* ruling. The Chinese brides of Chinese American soldiers were allowed into the United States, and Korean women arrived as wives of GIs back from the Korean War. Granted citizenship in return for their wartime service, Filipinos brought their families to America. The bars were lowered for Asian Indians. Though elements of the old quota system remained, an immigration law passed by Congress in 1952 eliminated the ban on naturalization for all Asians. Statehood for Hawaii in 1959 gave Asian Americans elected representatives in Washington.

But Asian Americans still ran into housing and job discrimination. They earned less on the average than did white Americans, even though a higher percentage of them had college degrees. With the intensification of the cold war, many white Americans also began to perceive them through an ideological as well as a racial prism.

Japanese Americans were now viewed favorably as Japan became America's key ally in Asia. But the fall of China to communism cast suspicion on Chinese Americans in the eyes of "Red hunters." President Lyndon B. Johnson, determined to make his Great Society even more progressive than Roosevelt's New Deal, launched sweeping civil rights programs. In 1965, at his behest, Congress passed the most liberal immigration act in history. Ending national origin quotas, it authorized the annual admission of 170,000 Asians and 120,000 Latin Americans in addition to those with close families already in America. The Communist

Growth of selected U.S. populations during the 1980s

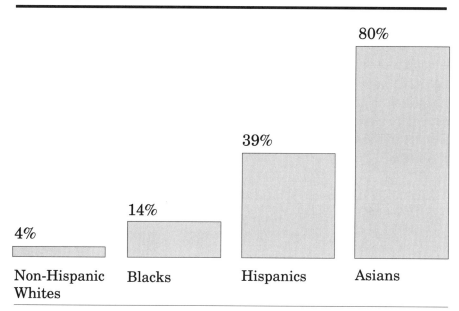

Source: Population Reference Bureau.

Asians as a percentage of all immigrants to the United States

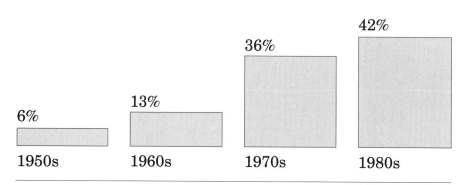

Source: U.S. Immigration and Naturalization Service.

conquest of Indochina in 1975 sparked a huge exodus of refugees, and Congress urgently voted legislation to admit them. During the 1980s, some 600,000 newcomers a year were legally arriving in the United States, more than 40 percent of them from Asia.

By 1990 immigration and births had expanded the number of Asian Americans to 7.3 million—a rate of growth double that of Hispanics, six times that of blacks, twenty times that of whites. Chinese Americans top the list, followed by Filipinos, Japanese, Indians, Koreans, Vietnamese, Laotians, Cambodians and Thais. Aside from Japanese Americans, most are immigrants. In one way or another, they are making an impact on America—and America is making an impact on them.

3

Family and Acculturation

A common characteristic of Asian Americans, whatever their heritage or land of origin, is the emphasis they place on family. Respect for elders and sacrifice for children figure prominently in shaping their experience. Whatever their national origin or ethnic or religious background—Buddhist, Hindu, Muslim, Sikh, or Christian—they prize education, hard work, thrift, obedience and respect for authority. Harmony is crucial, along with the notion that the group predominates over the individual. Their values in many ways embody the Puritan ethic that guided America's early settlers and was bequeathed to the successive generations that built the nation's institutions.

The image of Asian Americans as a "model minority," though inflated over time, was drawn from this parallel with Puritan values. The portrayal was conceived before the huge increase in the number of immigrants from Asia, and it has spawned the myth that all Asian Americans are free of the problems that trouble other groups. But Asian Americans do face racial discrimination, hate crimes, social problems and poverty. As they strive for acculturation, many are caught in the conflict traditionally experienced by immigrants: a clash between strong family values and permissive American ways. Thus they often feel alienated and isolated. Their experiences vary widely, however, by ethnicity, generation, education and region where they live. Refugees and immigrants, for example, encounter a variety of different difficulties than do second or third generation Asian Americans.

Whatever their backgrounds, Asian Americans share many traits. Only 5 percent live alone, while 76 percent live with their families. They marry later, and women are more likely to postpone childbearing until their thirties, even though their rate of childbirth is relatively high. The overwhelming majority of couples have children under the age of 15. Families also span generations. The proportion of grown children who live with their parents is five times higher among Asian Americans than in the total U.S. population, and the likelihood of an adult living with a brother or sister is nearly as great.

Teenage pregnancies are comparatively rare among Asian Americans. Children tend to stay in school and enter the labor force later. In 1990, two-thirds of Asian Americans between the ages of 16 and 24 attended school, significantly above the 54 percent for whites. School is likely to be the main activity for Asian American youngsters, reflecting the view of their parents that education is the ticket to social and economic success.

Because of the emphasis on education, parents foster close relations with their children, for whom they make huge sacrifices, often working day and night. For the sake of better schools for their offspring, Asian American families who can afford it move from inner-city pockets to suburban areas.

But Asian American refugee and poor immigrant families are often eroded by the necessity to work long hours and earn multiple incomes. A study conducted by the Asian Pacific Research and Development Council of the United Way in 1988 found "evidence of terrible and untold human need" among the Asian American communities of the San Gabriel Valley in Southern California. Among these problems are dysfunctional children, elderly people living in isolation, refugees exploited by sweatshops and adolescents turning to drugs and crime. Numbers of Vietnamese gang members, for example, are recruited among youths who have arrived in the United States alone, either because their families died during the Vietnam War or because they could not leave refugee camps. Unable to adapt to life in America, they quit school, encounter problems finding jobs and instead rob and extort. They in turn recruit other unadjusted youths.

Adapting to America puts tremendous pressure on other male refugees and immigrants. Accustomed to male-dominated cultures, they experience harsh role reversals and turmoil in their transplanted lives. Often their wives, who must work to make ends meet, find jobs more easily, and they frequently become more independent and assertive, thereby challenging their husbands. Rebellious children often defy their father's authority, which they regard as outmoded. The unquestioned obedience, duty and deference that they once paid to home and family breaks down.

For many adult refugees the loss of their country and relatives, coupled with the dilution of their identity in America, results in alcoholism as well as spouse and child abuse. Depression is a chronic mental health problem among numbers of Indochinese refugees, many of whom also suffer from nostalgia for their ancestral land. To seek professional counseling frequently violates the cultural sensibilities of Asian Americans, who traditionally shrink from discussing personal problems outside the family. Many also attach a stigma to mental illness, and their inclination to mask problems adds to the myth that they are free of trouble. This may rob them of social services. A number of organizations are seeking to help communities identify and cope with these problems.

Family pressure on children to excel in school is believed to be causing an increase in suicide among Asian American students, and the quiet, hard-working youngster depicted in the news media may in fact be a serious psychological case. A recent study by the U.S. Department of Health and Human Services reported that the rate of suicide among these young people has risen threefold during the past 20 years. The suicide rate among Chinese Americans between the ages of 15 and 24 was 36 percent greater than the national average, while that for Japanese Americans was 54 percent higher.

Other social problems bedevil Asian Americans as they try to cope with America. Hmong families, for example, frequently force daughters as young as 12 or 13 to marry. Some American public and child welfare agencies have labeled certain treatment of children as abusive when the real issue is cultural. School authorities have leveled charges against parents of Vietnamese children with suspicious-looking marks on their bodies, the result of a folkloric method of scraping the skin with a coin to rid the body of "bad vapors."

Asian Americans often strive to acculturate to the United States while retaining a sense of their roots. Even as second and third generation parents enter the American mainstream and move to the suburbs, they attempt to instill in their children a knowledge and appreciation of their ancestry. Three hours once a week, for example, Chinese American students arrive at Irvine Chinese School in Orange County, California, where they learn to speak Mandarin, memorize Confucian adages and listen to lectures on Chinese history. Vietnamese communities conduct classes in Vietnamese language and culture for their children. These practices help to reinforce and provide a context for values taught at home.

Holidays are invariably bicultural. New Year's is celebrated twice by Chinese Americans, first according to the Western and then in conformity with the Chinese lunar calendar. Just as St. Patrick's Day is marked by an annual parade, Deepavali, the Indian festival of lights, is celebrated in New York by a fair organized by Indian Americans. The California cities of Alhambra and Monterey Park joined for the first time in 1992 to herald the Year of the Monkey. Thanksgiving turkey might be accompanied by dim sum, sushi or curry. Weddings may mean costume changes for brides, who appear in both lacy white gowns and kimonos and *ao dais*. There is an Americanized version of the traditional Japanese cherry blossom festival in San Francisco, and the annual Nisei week in Los Angeles is a similar blend.

But many Asian Americans have become as American as apple pie. Debutantes come out at cotillions, young men root for their favorite football teams and college students belong to sororities and fraternities. They organize beauty pageants, and some Asian American women are winning their tiaras in big events. For example, in 1981 Leslie Kawai, a Japanese American, was crowned Rose Queen in the Tournament of Roses in Pasadena.

Americanization can dilute traditional values. Educational performance declines and divorce rises with the second, third and fourth generations. Despite family pressures, many young Asian Americans are abandoning such secure and lucrative professions as medicine, science and engineering for risky fields like literature and the arts. A recent *Time* article describing their eagerness to dispel the image of themselves as whiz kids was headlined: "Kicking the Nerd Syndrome."

More successful than men in breaking the mold, Asian American women are getting high-profile jobs in television and politics. Women appear to adapt rapidly, a lesson learned in Asian households where males, notably first sons, are held in high esteem. Mothers dote on fathers and sons, and wives on husbands. Girls are not entirely neglected, yet boys are usually the focus of attention, especially in families that perpetuate traditional patriarchal values. Family pampering leaves some Asian American men uncomfortable in aggressive American situations.

Nowhere is the difference between Asian American men and women more visible as they integrate into the United States than in their marriage behavior. Asian American women seem to select spouses outside their own ethnic group at a faster rate than men. The mixed marriage rate among Asian Americans is increasing rapidly. Interracial couples already make up an estimated 10 to 15 percent of these marriages. Japanese Americans are in the forefront of the trend, with more than half marrying outside their group—mostly with whites. Americans of Filipinos origin come next, followed by Chinese, Vietnamese and Korean Americans.

Asian American families, like other American families, face myriad challenges. But though they are under pressure, their unique solidarity is, for the present, the foundation for their ability to benefit from the opportunities offered by the United States.

Characteristics of Asian-Americans by Country of Origin

	Percentage of Asian American population	Percentage foreign born	Percentage who do not speak English well	Percentage who live in the West
Chinese	22.6	63.3	23	52.7
Filipino	19.3	64.7	6	68.8
Japanese	11.6	28.4	9	80.3
Asian Indian	11.2	70.4	5	19.2
Korean	11.0	81.9	24	42.9
Vietnamese	8.4	90.5	38	46.2
Lao	2.0	93.7	69	45.7
Thai	1.3	82.1	12	43.0
Cambodian	2.0	93.9	59	55.6
Hmong	1.2	90.5	63	37.4
Pakistani	–	85.1	10	23.5
Indonesian	–	83.4	6	56.2
All Asian-Americans	**100.0**	**62.1**	**15**	**56.4**

Source: U.S. Bureau of the Census, *We, the Asian and Pacific Islander Americans*, p.11, table 7, and U.S. General Accounting Office, *Asian Americans: A Status Report*, p. 44, table 6.1.

4

Education

The sacrifice, diligence and determination of Asian American parents produce extraordinary results in the educational accomplishments of their children, who are performing at high standards of excellence and posing new challenges for the academic establishment. But the achievements are mixed. Though young Asian Americans win school prizes, many feel confined to the fields of science, math and engineering, which could narrow their future careers. While their enrollment at prestigious universities is proportionately greater than their presence in the population, many of them believe that their admission to college is curbed by quotas that disregard their merit. The statistical evidence is also clear that Asian Americans are bumping against a glass ceiling as they strive for faculty and administrative appointments.

Asian American students often claim that school officials neglect them unless they conform to the stereotype of nerdy math and science wizards and avoid the humanities and liberal arts. The conventional image of them as unalloyed successes further obscures the fact that 20 percent of them have not finished high school, a rate slightly above that for whites. This is particularly true for recent immigrants. As Shirley Hune, associate provost of Hunter College of the City University of New York, has said, "There is woefully inadequate attention and resources to assure that they become proficient in English."

Studies of Asian Americans consistently link their performance in school to family encouragement and cohesion. Researchers have even discovered that immigrant children who speak their native language at home do exceptionally well in class because they are communicating with their parents, whose approval they seek to gain. The consistent emphasis on learning at home and in school helps to obscure differences between the two environments. By contrast, dropouts often come from troubled home situations. Many teenage Chinese and Vietnamese gang members, for instance, are youngsters who arrived in the United States without their families.

For many young Asian Americans, the desire to excel is also a consequence of pressure at home, where families often lean on them relentlessly to succeed at the most illustrious schools—a tradition that for some stems from the Confucian emphasis on rising to the upper echelons of the bureaucracy through education. Some Asian families emigrate to the United States solely for the purpose of getting their offspring into prestigious schools, and many more work hard to keep them there. Allan Chin, a Chinese American and a leading radiation expert, whose father ran a laundry in Roxbury, Massachusetts, has recalled: "It's amazing. The laundry enabled him to raise seven children and put them all through college."

But family expectations can be excessive. In Los Angeles not long ago, a Korean American was sentenced to six months in jail for beating his daughter because her grade point average was 3.83 rather than a perfect 4.0. Such extreme examples among immigrant families are rare, but an increasing number of Asian American students, unable to withstand such parental pressures, commit suicide.

More often, Asian American youths fulfill the dreams of their families. They have regularly outshined other groups in the math section of the Scholastic Aptitude Test and ranked second only to whites in the verbal portion. During the 1980s, they won one in four of the Westinghouse Science Talent Search scholarships awarded to high school students, and in 1991 they were 18 of the 40 finalists in the competition. Not a spring goes by without Vietnamese refugee children appearing as valedictorians at their high school graduation ceremonies.

Moreover, 40 percent of Asian Americans hold college degrees, compared to 21 percent for Americans as a whole. Alleged quotas notwithstanding, their college admission rate has been spectacular. Asian Americans in freshmen classes in 1991 ranged from 19 percent at Harvard to 51 percent at the Irvine campus of the University of California. The numbers are similar in terms of their overall undergraduate presence. In 1991 they constituted 18 percent of the student body at Stanford and 22 percent at the Massachusetts Institute of Technology. But, like Americans as a whole, not all attend top schools, and many of them attend public community colleges.

The change in campus demographics is provoking concerns about a possible backlash. Some white students have spread the line that UCLA—the University of California at Los Angeles—should be called "United Caucasians Living among Asians," and MIT has been dubbed "Made in Taiwan." In some colleges, as the number of Asian Americans has risen, so have the graffiti and hate mail decrying their presence.

The increased number of Asian Americans in the 1991 freshman classes at many major universities followed charges that quotas were being imposed to limit their enrollment. In 1987 Yat-Pang Au, a star graduate of Jose Gunderson High School in San Jose, California, was denied admission to the University of California at Berkeley. The incident sparked a controversy in the state and elsewhere in the country, prompting his and other Asian American parents whose children had been rejected to complain of discrimination to the Department of Justice. Their protest raised the issue of whether quotas, however disguised, did indeed exist. It also evoked comparisons between qualified Asian Americans and top Jewish American candidates rebuffed as "damned curve raisers" by Ivy League schools during the 1920s and 1930s.

A study has shown that Asian Americans entered the nation's universities at roughly the same rate as whites until the middle of the 1980s, after which their admissions dropped. The enrollment of whites also declined at the time, but the drop in Asian Americans was steeper. This was the case in California, which has the nation's largest Asian American population. Since then the admission of Asian Americans has again increased, suggesting that the trend was temporary. But what happened is still a subject of debate.

Many Asian Americans have maintained that they were not consulted about changes in admissions policies that reduced the influence of grades and test scores, their chief strength, and put a greater stress on such extracurricular activities as sports and campus politics, on which they put less emphasis. At the same time, the number of low-income Asian Americans admitted under affirmative action was scaled back.

Investigations and legislative hearings have concluded that no actual quotas existed, but Asian Americans educators disagree. Their complaints, among others, led to an array of surveys. The U.S. Department of Education's Civil Rights Office launched a "compliance review" of admissions policies and practices at UCLA, Berkeley, Harvard and other institutions in 1988. A year later, the federal office began a probe into allegations by an Asian American student that Berkeley's affirmative action program constituted an illegal quota that, by favoring blacks and Hispanics, diminished the chances of other groups. The authorities at Berkeley meanwhile reappraised their policies.

These investigations have produced a variety of conclusions. The Department of Education found that Harvard, which gives priority to the sons and daughters of alumni, was not discriminatory. But it concluded that UCLA's graduate math program had discriminated against five Asian Americans, and it is now looking into the university's undergraduate admissions procedures as well as those at Berkeley. In 1989 a committee at Berkeley acknowledged that, while no quotas had been imposed to limit Asian American freshmen, some earlier admissions policies had hurt their chances. Other universities have since reviewed and altered their admission policies to treat Asian Americans more fairly, and the rise in enrollments reflects these adjustments.

The effect of affirmative action on Asian Americans continues to be debated. Like the students, Asian American faculty members are chiefly concentrated in math, science and engineering, which has prompted the American Council on Education to recommend that universities examine tenure and hiring practices to determine the causes of their underrepresentation in other fields. But they have been prominent in Asian American studies, which like women's and black studies surfaced during the civil rights movement and student unrest of the 1960s, when minorities were asserting their identity. Berkeley and San Francisco State University were among the first to offer courses in Asian American studies and others have followed suit, providing valuable research on the subject. But they must compete for resources and, as Shirley Hune has noted, their legitimacy "is still very much in question."

Asian American activists rallied behind Don Nakanishi, a Japanese American who waged a three-year fight for tenure at the UCLA Graduate School of Education. Nakanishi had earned his undergraduate degree at Yale and his doctorate in political science at Harvard before becoming an assistant professor at UCLA. His supporters cast him as a victim of prejudice and ultraconservative scholarship and depicted him as a symbol of ethnic and intellectual diversity at an American university. His critics questioned the quality of his research on Asian American voting patterns and college admissions, arguing that it was below UCLA's standards. Nakanishi claimed they had no basis for understanding his work and thus dismissed it as marginal. His fight became a cause célèbre for Asian American and other minority activists, who raised money and mobilized support for his struggle. He finally won tenure in 1989 and was later appointed director of UCLA's Asian American Studies Center.

But though Nakanishi's case was highly publicized, it was not the only instance of such a challenge to academic policies and practices. Rosalie Tung, a Chinese American, sued the Wharton School of Business at the University of Pennsylvania, charging race and sexual discrimination in the denial of her tenure in 1985. The university refused to open its tenure file, contending that academic freedom would be compromised. Though the suit is still pending, the U.S. Supreme Court ruled in 1990 that she was entitled to see her file. That year, Jean Jew, also a Chinese American and a professor at the University of Iowa College School of Medicine, won a $1 million award after suing for discrimination. Mark Tanouye, a Japanese American, settled a similar suit against the California Institute of Technology for denying him tenure. Even before the suit was settled, however, he received tenure offers from other universities and chose Berkeley.

Not all Asian Americans have been as successful, however, and as a group they rank low in tenured jobs. Women among them, like women of every background, trail men in prominent positions. As Shirley Hune has remarked, "What is a glass ceiling for Asian American males is a cement floor for Asian American women."

Many educational officials submit that Asian Americans will have only a minimal impact on university procedures as long as they remain in laboratories and shun the arts and humanities, fields that would give them a voice in the formulation of policy. They cite the example of the late S. I. Hayakawa, a distinguished linguistics expert who became the controversial president of San Francisco State before his election to the U.S. Senate. But a notable exception is Chang-Lin Tien, a mechanical engineer born in China, who in 1990 was appointed chancellor of Berkeley, one of America's largest universities.

Even so, Asian American academic administrators are rare. Bob Suzuki, a Japanese American, heads California State Polytechnic University, Pomona, and Jack Fujimoto presides over Mission College, a community college in Sylmar near Los Angeles. Shirley Hune is one of the few Asian American women to have climbed to the policy-making level. Moreover, the number of Asian American administrators and faculty members lags far behind that of Asian American university students. At UCLA, for instance, the size of the Asian American student body doubled between 1980 and 1990, yet few Asian American professors were hired during that decade—and they now make up only 7 percent of the faculty. The top 71 administrators at UCLA include only two Asian Americans. All this despite the fact that both Asian Americans and foreign-born Asians in the United States earned proportionately more advanced degrees than any other group. Despite the obstacles confronting them, Asian American women have been in the vanguard of this trend. One out of every 14 women dentists in America is of Asian descent, as are 20 percent of female medical doctors—twice the number of black and Hispanic physicians combined.

That Asian Americans must overcome an assortment of problems in the academic community is evident. But their progress in education until now, though sometimes inflated by the news media, has been noteworthy—and there is every reason to believe that it will continue.

Educational Attainment

Percentage of persons 25 and over with four or more years of college, 1990

Asian-Americans	40%
Non-Hispanic whites	23%
Blacks	12%
Hispanics	10%
All U.S.	21%

Percentage of 1980 high school seniors who earned a bachelor's degree by February 1986

Asian-Americans	20%
Non-Hispanic whites	21%
Blacks	10%
Hispanics	7%
All U.S.	19%

Source: U.S. Bureau of the Census and U.S. National Center for Education Statistics.

5

Culture and Arts

The Asian American experience is a fusion of cultures that belies Rudyard Kipling's famous line, "East is East and West is West and never the twain shall meet." Asian American writers and artists are capturing their unique experience in books, films, plays, arts and music. Their work defies the image of "oriental" exotica most familiar to American readers and audiences.

Asian Americans are expressing themselves in new and rich forms, creating self portraits that contribute to an awareness of Asians in America extending beyond such clichés as Japanese prints, Kung Fu movies and trendy Thai food. Their quest for self-definition is not new, but for years their artistic expressions have been recognized primarily by Asian American audiences. Now, finally, Asian American writers and artists are gathering a wider, national audience. Their work, often a complex blend of Asian heritage and expression, eludes easy definition.

Until recently, it was chiefly whites who conveyed the Asian image to mainstream America. Their characterizations often fostered negative, racist stereotypes of Asian Americans that persisted for more than a century—and still do even as Asian Americans broaden their roles in entertainment, sports, politics and the news media. Many believe that Americans as a whole must discard distortions of the past and rediscover the realities of Asian Americans.

Elaine Kim, a professor at the University of California at Berkeley, has noted that "one of the fundamental barriers to understanding and appreciating Asian American literary self-expression has been the existence of race stereotypes. . . . Probably more Americans know Fu Manchu and Charlie Chan than know Asians or Asian American human beings. Even the elite culture shares the popular stereotypes." Frank Chin, a contemporary Chinese American playwright, has suggested that critics of his "Chickencoop Chinaman," staged in New York in the early 1970s, failed to grasp his characters because they did not speak, dress or act like "Orientals."

Images personifying Asians have ranged from menacing "yellow peril" portraits in cartoons to caricatures of them as exotic and inscrutable. Fu Manchu, the sinister Chinese invented by the British author Sax Rohmer, typified evil "in every twitch of his finger and terror in each split second of his slanted eyes." By contrast, the Chinese detective Charlie Chan dispensed wisdom in tonal English with such fortune cookie homilies as "theory, like mist on eyeglasses, obscures fact." Created by Earl Derr Biggers in 1925, he later appeared in dozens of books and nearly 50 films, whose producers hoped to refute the Fu Manchu image. John Marquand's sleuth, Mr. Moto, was a Japanese version of Charlie Chan. Pearl Buck, the daughter of missionaries to China, made Americans weep with *The Good Earth*, her 1932 Pulitzer Prize–winning fantasy of China's stoic peasants.

In the past, Hollywood invariably cast whites as Asians. Pearl Buck's peasants were depicted on the screen by Paul Muni and Louise Rainier, both Austrian Jews. Warner Oland played Charlie Chan, Peter Lorre was Mr. Moto, Yul Brunner gained fame as the king of Siam and Marlon Brando was Sakini in "Teahouse of the August Moon." Even Mickey Rooney got into the act as a myopic, bucktoothed Japanese photographer in "Breakfast at Tiffany's." As a result, they eclipsed many talented, available Asian American actors.

A few Asian Americans have distinguished themselves on the screen. Anna May Wong, an exquisite ingenue of Chinese origin, went on to wicked roles. A popular romantic lead in silent films, Sessue Hayakawa, was later a candidate for an Academy Award for his rendition of the Japanese commander in "The Bridge on the River Kwai." The movie of James Michener's "Sayonara" included Miyoshi Umeki, who won an Oscar as best supporting actress. Haing G. Ngor also earned an Academy Award for his debut in "The Killing Fields," and Mako was nominated for the prize for his part in "Sand Pebbles."

Even so, Asian Americans have seldom been featured in films. They are usually servants, like Inspector Clouseau's bumbling Cato in the "Pink Panther" series, or villains like Oddjob in "Goldfinger." They have been the enemy in movies about World War II, the Korean conflict and Vietnam. But not all Asian Americans play predictable roles. George Takei, best known as Captain Sulu in the original "Star Trek" television series and its film sequels, is simply a space-age figure. Similarly Pat Morita played a television detective in "Ohara." Joan Chen was one of the offbeat characters in "Twin Peaks."

Broadway plays with Asian themes, such as "Flower Drum Song" and "Pacific Overtures," have long attracted American audiences. All were the work of white Americans until David Henry Hwang, a Chinese American, came along with "M. Butterfly," which earned the 1988 Tony award and established him as a leading American playwright. The play is about a French diplomat, Gallimard, who discovers that Song, his Chinese mistress of 20 years, is actually a man to whom he has been confiding state secrets. The Frenchman claims during his trial for treason that he did not know Song's true gender. Hwang's work explores the West's attitudes— often condescending and racist—toward the East.

Actor B. D. Wong also won a Tony for his role as the mistress in the drama. But such choice roles are rare, and the frustration of many Asian Americans in the theater erupted in 1990 in a controversy over casting the musical "Miss Saigon." Hwang and Wong both protested the choice of British actor Jonathan Pryce to play a Eurasian pimp in the Broadway production. Other Asian Americans joined them, arguing that an Asian American deserved the part. The protest fizzled when the producer threatened to scrap the show, yet it did have an impact. An Asian American actor, Francis Ruivivar, succeeded Pryce after ten months. "In my opinion," B.D. Wong later remarked, "he never would have been considered for that part if there wasn't a big fuss over it."

Commenting on the flap in a recent interview, director, writer and actor Peter Wang put it in a different perspective. "It never occurred to me in my wildest dreams to play Shakespeare," he said. "His plays are wonderful to see and study, but what has that got to do with me? I don't look like Hamlet. I'd rather play a hero in Chinese history, a Qing dynasty emperor or general. But we must come out and yell, and make our voices heard, our identities recognized."

To create greater and more interesting TV and movie roles, Asian American actors, playwrights and directors are increasingly striving to project an Asian presence into American culture, and some have succeeded in creating sensitive portrayals of Asian Americans. Pat Morita lent special sensitivity to "Karate Kid," during a scene recalling the Japanese American internment experience. Mako and Nobu McCarthy played a Japanese American couple in a disintegrating marriage in the film version of "The Wash," written by Philip Kan Gotanda and directed by Michael T. Uno. Peter Wang, a former professor of engineering born in China, focused on the Chinese American experience in "A Great Wall," as did director Wayne Wang in "Dim Sum."

Until now, Asian Americans have chiefly found recognition in local theater groups such as the East-West Players in Los Angeles and New York's Pan Asian Repertory Theater. They have produced works distinguished for their Asian American point of view like Jude Narita's "Song for a Sansei" and Amy Hill's "Tokyo Bound." Lane Nishikawa's "Life in the Fast Lane" was the first one-person show written and acted by an Asian American.

One of Hollywood's most distinguished cameramen was the late James Wong Howe, an American born in China. Many Asian Americans have followed in his footsteps as the figures behind movie and stage productions. Visual Communications, founded in 1970 and the country's oldest Asian American media arts center, has produced such early Asian American films as "Cruisin' J-Town" and "Piece of a Dream." The National Asian American Telecommunications Association has been instrumental in helping Asian American production groups to get funding. An independent Japanese American filmmaker, Steve Okazaki, won an Oscar in 1991 for his documentary "Days of Waiting."

An impressive development has been the recent surge of Asian American writers. As *Publishers Weekly* commented not long ago: "Perhaps not since the mainstream 'discovered' Jewish American fiction in the 1950s has such a concentrated, seemingly 'new' ethnic literary wave come our way."

Edith Eaton, a Eurasian who adopted the pen name Sui Sin Far and died in 1914, was probably the first Asian American to write in English about Asians in the United States. Early Chinese newcomers composed verses in Chinese, several of which have been translated by Him Mark Lai, Genny Lim and Judy Yung in *Island: Poetry and History of Chinese Immigrants on Angel Island*. Pioneer accounts of Japanese Americans are Etsu Sugimoto's *A Daughter of a Samurai*, published in 1925, and the writings of Hisaye Yamamoto and Toshio Mori. The Filipino American writer Carlos Bulosan also evoked his experiences in the United States during the

1930s in his eloquent *America is in the Heart*. But not until after World War II did the memoir of an Asian American have the impact of Jade Snow Wong's *Fifth Chinese Daughter*, which chronicled her adjustment to American life. The same theme, in various forms, has preoccupied the latest tide of Asian American writers.

Maxine Hong Kingston attracted a big American audience with *The Woman Warrior*, published in 1976, and she has since become a major American literary figure. Amy Tan's *The Joy Luck Club* was a bestseller, as was her second novel, *The Kitchen God's Wife*. Other acclaimed Asian American writers include Gish Jen, Gus Lee, Cynthia Kadohata, Bette Bao Lord, Bharati Mukherjee and Jessica Hagedorn. Some have been derided by Asian American rivals who accuse them of pandering to the mainstream. Other Asian American writers fear that their work will be judged chiefly for its ethnic singularity rather than as art. Amy Tan, who has been criticized by other Asian Americans for depicting characters whose English is flawed, has explained, "I saw people who were without the voice to tell their stories and who, like myself, grew up thinking that their thoughts were worthless because they didn't speak good English." Yet she also feels some frustration that her work is viewed through a cultural prism. "There is something about language and the qualities of storytelling, or the quality of characterizations, that gets more ignored with a writer who has an ethnicity different from the so-called mainstream."

Asian Americans are also writing about economics, politics and current affairs. In 1981 Professor William G. Ouchi of UCLA published the bestseller *Theory Z*, on how American business could cope with the challenge of Japan. Francis Fukuyama's *The End of History and The Last Man* appeared in 1992, and Grant Ujifusa is the co-author with Michael Barone of the annual *Almanac of American Politics*. Asian American scholars are reaching beyond purely academic works to relate the Asian American story to the public, as evidenced by Berkeley Professor Ronald Takaki's *Strangers from Another Shore*. The history of Asian Americans is being preserved as well in museums and other institutions.

In 1992 the Japan American National Museum opened in the Little Tokyo district of downtown Los Angeles. The district also has a memorial to Ellison Onizuka, the Japanese American astronaut killed in the explosion of the Challenger in 1986. The Manzanar internment camp near Independence, California, is to be officially upgraded to a national historical site, and the Japanese Americans uprooted during World War II are being remembered in other ways, including an exhibition at the Smithsonian Institution in Washington, D.C. Chinese Americans have been evoking their past with Chinese American Historical Societies in the Chinatowns of San Francisco and New York. Many are seeking to refurbish Angel Island, where Chinese immigrants were detained early in the century, as Ellis Island has been. The Filipino American Historical Society, based in Seattle, has branches around the country.

Asian American contributions to the arts are visible everywhere. I. M. Pei, who was born in China, is the world's foremost architect. Maya Lin, another Chinese American, designed the Vietnam War Memorial in Washington and the new Civil Rights monument in Montgomery, Alabama. Yet another Chinese American, Dong Kingman, is a leading painter and illustrator. The late Isamu Noguchi, a Japanese American, was one of this nation's most creative sculptors.

Asian Americans are figuring prominently in music as well. Cellist Yo Yo Ma, along with conductors Zubin Mehta and Seiji Ozawa, are concert favorites, and Asian Americans are heavily represented at the Juilliard School. Hiroshima was the first Asian American pop/jazz group to sign with a major record company. Singer Don Ho has entertained Hawaii for years, and Asian Americans are becoming jazz buffs. A rising pop figure is Kim Tsoy, a Korean American who bills himself the Eastern Cowboy. His country-and- western combo, Next of Kin, is popular throughout the South. Elvis Presley lives on in Elvis Phuong, a Vietnamese American rock singer.

Sports is another American frontier being crossed by Asian Americans. Sammy Lee, a Korean American, won Olympic gold medals for diving in 1948 and 1952. Victoria Draves, a Filipino American diver, won a gold medal in 1948. Kristi Yamaguchi, the Japanese American skater, was the Olympic gold medalist in 1992. Other American world-class skaters of Asian descent include Natasha Kuchiki, Tiffany Chin and Tai Babilonia. Michael Chang is one of America's top tennis pros, and Corey Nakatani is a leading jockey.

Asian Americans may feel that they still have a long way to go before they are fully accepted on the American cultural scene. But they have come a long distance over the past generation in an area that, ideally, has no boundaries.

6

Economics

The economic status of Asian Americans is as disparate as the group itself, varying by generation, education, employment and origin. Many third and fourth generation Chinese and Japanese Americans have risen into professional ranks, while numbers of newcomers, especially from Southeast Asia, struggle with poverty and depend on welfare. But even those who are highly qualified often find themselves blocked from climbing to the heights of corporate America, and have started their own firms—frequently with much success.

Despite their diversity, Asian Americans as a whole are seen by major American enterprises as avid and affluent consumers, so that companies ranging from Metropolitan Life to American Telephone & Telegraph pitch their services and products in special bilingual promotions and advertisements.

The economic profile of Asian Americans is far more complex than the statistics indicate. Home ownership, one measure of wealth, shows considerable variations. Only 54 percent of Asian Americans owned their homes in 1990, compared to 74 percent for white Americans. The figure has remained almost unchanged over the past decade, indicating that the accumulation of assets by Asian Americans is probably not as high as generally perceived. But many of those who spend on housing spend lavishly, as evidenced by their suburban mansions around Los Angeles and New York. The average value of homes owned by Asian Americans in 1987 was $136,800, more than double that of white-owned houses.

Their diversity also makes it difficult to generalize about the earnings of Asian Americans. Though their median family income in 1989 was a relatively high $35,900, they are largely clustered in expensive metropolitan areas like Los Angeles and New York, where they may not be as well off as their earnings suggest. The multiplicity of wage earners in their households is somewhat greater than the national average, which explains their lower per capita income—an average of $14,000 a year in 1989, compared to $14,700 for whites. The earnings of assorted Asian American groups differ drastically, thereby skewing averages. The median family income of Chinese Americans in 1980, for example, was four times higher than that of Laotian families. Japanese, Indian and Filipino American household incomes are well above the national average, while those of Korean and Vietnamese descent are below it. Each group has rich and poor.

The term "immigrant," which summons up an image of destitution, can be misleading. There are recent Chinese arrivals from Hong Kong whose incomes surpass those of most white Americans and other Chinese newcomers who work in garment factories for miserable wages. Many of the Vietnamese who landed in America after the Communist conquest of Vietnam in 1975 were entrepreneurs and professionals who have done well since, while the peasants, fisherfolk and former political prisoners who followed in later years have had a tougher time of it economically. Poverty is particularly prevalent among the subsequent Indochinese refugees, most of them known as "boat people," who make up roughly 40 percent of the immigrants from Vietnam during the 1980s. The poverty rate of Asian Americans as a whole rose to 14 percent in 1989, about twice that of whites, which had been falling—at least prior to the 1990–92 recession.

Needy Asian Americans are more likely than whites to draw on public assistance. While Asian Americans comprised three percent of the poverty population by 1989, nearly 60 percent of impoverished Asian American households used public assistance, food stamps or low-income energy assistance, a rate 10 percent higher than that for white families. Poor Asian Americans are drawn to California because of the warm climate and large, established Asian communities. But the state also is attractive because of its generous welfare programs.

Older Asian Americans, under the pressure of making ends meet, often retire later than do whites. Many are recent immigrants who have contributed little to Social Security, and that discourages them from retiring as well. In 1989 their mean Social Security income was $5,300, compared to $5,800 for whites. Staying in the work force longer may account for the low unemployment rate among Asian Americans, which was 3.5 percent in 1990, nearly half the national average. Classifying their job status can be complicated, however. Numbers who work part-time in family enterprises fail to report (or underreport) their incomes for tax and other reasons, as do the thousands of waiters, dishwashers and seamstresses in urban enclaves like Chinatown.

Between 1982 and 1987, Asian Americans outpaced every group in the country in establishing new enterprises, whose combined revenues during the period soared by 162 percent, compared to a national average increase of 14 percent. These enterprises come in every size and shape, from mom and pop businesses to big companies, and different groups have their specialities: Indian Americans run hotels and motels, Korean Americans operate grocery stores and service stations, and Cambodian Americans in California tend toward doughnut shops. The Chinese restaurant has been an American institution for more than a century.

Several factors underline this entrepreneurial trend. Numbers of Asian Americans are recent immigrants who feel handicapped by their inadequate English. Though many are well educated and skilled, they find themselves stymied in large corporations, which often refuse to promote them. Many also start their own businesses because they can obtain interest-free loans from informal family and clan credit unions, like the *tanomoshi* created by early Japanese settlers and the *kye*, which still serves Korean newcomers. They are frequently comfortable as well when they can employ trustworthy members of their family. But reliance on family is not always the path to success. Wang Laboratories, one of the pioneers in America's computer industry, began to slide because its founder, the late An Wang, insisted on bequeathing its direction to his son.

It would be a distortion, however, to deny the success of some Asian Americans in major American companies. Once again, though, their accomplishments vary by group. Indian and Chinese Americans, for instance, outpace whites in the proportion of management positions they hold. Shirley Young, an American of Chinese origin, is a vice president of General Motors, and Anne Shen Smith, also of Chinese origin, is a top executive at Southern California Edison. Sirjang Lal Tandon, who came to the United States from India, is chairman, president and chief executive of Tandon Corporation. Safi U. Qureshey, an immigrant from Pakistan, heads AST Research. Asian Americans are prized by corporations that do business with Asia. Thus Gareth C. Chang is vice president for McDonnell

Douglas's Asian operations and Robert Nakasone is vice chairman of Toys R Us, which is active in Japan.

Nevertheless, barriers to advancement still exist even at companies with heavy concentrations of Asian American employees. At Hughes Aircraft, for example, where they account for 25 percent of the engineers, Asian Americans are conspicuously absent from senior management. Only one of the seven group vice presidents is Asian American. David Barclay, a vice president at Hughes, recently noted that Asian American engineers and technicians, possibly out of frustration, are leaving the company just as they are hitting their stride. As he put it, "We are beginning to lose them in the technical area in the four-to-seven-year range, when they start to think about promotion. And if those promotions are not occurring, they consider moving on." Silicon Valley, among other areas, is testimony to the numbers of Asian Americans who did in fact move on to create their own firms, often with financing from friends in places like Hong Kong and Taiwan.

A question is whether the influence of traditional values deters Asian Americans from moving upward in the workplace. David Barclay has observed that Asian Americans tend to be clannish, so that, as he remarked not long ago, "If we have a Japanese manager, that department has been loaded with Japanese. If we have a Korean manager, it is Korean. Chinese, it's Chinese." At the same time, Asian Americans are often not perceived as aggressive enough by corporate America, and many are indeed reluctant to promote themselves directly—a practice that goes against the grain of

Economic Indicators

	Median Family Income	Average number of earners per family	Unemployment rate	Poverty rate
Asian-Americans	35,900	1.8	3.5	14%
Non-Hispanic whites	35,000	1.7	4.2	8%
Hispanics	23,400	1.7	10.3	26%
Blacks	20,200	1.5	12.3	31%
All U.S.	34,200	1.7	6.8	13%

Source: U.S. Bureau of Labor Statistics. U.S. Bureau of the Census. Population Reference Bureau Data for years 1989 (cols. 1, 2, and 4) and 1990 (col. 3).

Percentage of entrepreneurs among Asian-Americans

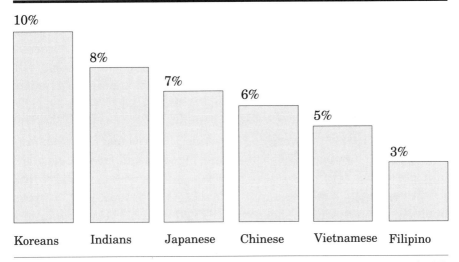

10%	8%	7%	6%	5%	3%
Koreans	Indians	Japanese	Chinese	Vietnamese	Filipino

Source: Estimates by Professor William O'Hare, University of Louisville, from U.S. Bureau of the Census data for 1987.

Businesses owned by Asian-Americans

	1977	1987
Japanese	27,000	53,000
Chinese	23,000	90,000
Filipino	10,000	40,000
Korean	9,000	69,000
Indian	7,000	52,000
Other	7,000	25,000
Total	83,000	355,000

Source: U.S. Bureau of the Census.

Occupations

Percentage holding professional or managerial jobs

Indians	47%
Chinese	30%
Japanese	28%
Koreans	22%
Whites	24%

Source: U.S. Bureau of the Census, data from 1980 Census.

many Asian cultures.

The Leadership Education for Asian Pacifics, a Los Angeles group, is guiding Asian Americans employed by U.S. companies by providing management training, and it is also trying to sensitize American companies by conducting cultural awareness programs about Asian Americans for their managers. A similar program functions under the auspices of the Asian American Manufacturers Association, an organization of high-tech entrepreneurs, which seeks to expand the skills and knowledge of Asian Americans employed by large U.S. firms.

Yet another question worth examining is whether Asian Americans ought to want to work for big American companies, given the inequities in their wages. Despite their sterling academic credentials, they earn less on average than whites with comparable educations. Those with college degrees earned a median annual income of $23,000, while a white employee with the same diploma made $25,200. And advanced education does not appear to narrow the salary discrepancy. The earnings of Asian Americans rose an average of $2,300 a year for every additional year of university completed, while whites gained almost $3,000 more. A similar pattern prevails for Asian American women, who trail not only Asian American men but white males and females as well.

One consequence of wage and other forms of discrimination has been a chorus of complaints by Asian Americans, many of whom have lodged suits against employers. According to Margaret Fung of the Asian American Legal Defense and Education Fund, a New York group, they include scientists, doctors, bankers and administrators. As she put it, "We hear the same grievances again and again—that they come in at entry-level jobs, but the white employees hired at the same time have received promotions while they remain in technical or low managerial positions."

The positive side is that Asian Americans, despite hurdles, have been steadily improving their status. In the process, many have learned that education alone is no guarantee of better jobs, nor are promotions based solely on merit. The key to future success, many realize, is to acquire new skills that will help them to vault barriers. As it is, they have already made dramatic contributions to the U.S. economy—which, as it seeks to regain its former strength, would benefit from more of their talent, dynamism and innovation.

7

Discrimination and Violence

A *Wall Street Journal* survey in May 1991 found that most Americans do not believe that Asian Americans face racial bigotry, and some even contend that they are granted "too many special advantages." Thus the general public sees Asian Americans as an untroubled "model minority."

But Asian Americans are confronted by prejudice, though much of it may be subtle. A majority of Asian Americans polled in southern California by the *Los Angeles Times* in January 1989 replied that discrimination denies them jobs and promotions. Other studies show that Asian Americans do not always have equal access to higher education, health care and other public services. They have also been slurred by figures like *Newsday* columnist Jimmy Breslin, who called a female Korean American colleague a "yellow cur," and John Silber, the Democratic candidate for governor of Massachusetts in 1990, who decried the town of Lowell, which is heavily populated by Cambodian refugees, as a "welfare magnet" that has "suddenly become popular for people . . . accustomed to living in a tropical climate." Asian Americans are often the victims of violence, not only from whites and other minorities but from Asian gangs. Numbers of newcomers exploited by their bosses are ignored by labor officials, so that discrimination can also take the shape of indifference.

Racism is a global phenomenon. Its liberal tradition notwithstanding, France recently voted heavily for a racist and chauvinistic political party. Germany is haunted by a neo-Nazi resurgence, extremists are emerging in Switzerland and Sweden, Britain limits the admission of Africans and Asians. Caste pervades India and social status in the Philippines is based on color. Not only does Japan discriminate against its Korean minority and the indigenous Ainu, but prominent Japanese derogate African and Hispanic Americans.

Though racism has long been an American dilemma as well, it does not entirely account for the difficulties of Asian Americans. Many are recent immigrants from lands governed by autocratic regimes, and despite strenuous efforts by advocacy groups to aid them, they cannot understand their rights under the American legal system. Newcomers often view themselves as "guests" who ought to express gratitude to their host country rather than voice their grievances. Reluctant to consult strangers, they also distrust welfare agencies and prefer instead to confide in sympathetic but unqualified relatives and friends.

Whatever their shortcomings, the notion that they are all successful deprives many of the assistance they need to adapt to America. So the model minority stereotype, originally intended to be a tribute to their hard work and perseverance, can be an affliction in disguise.

Even those whose forebears have been in the United States for generations encounter discrimination, racial epithets and even attacks. More often, though, they are subjected to oblique forms of bias, such as when other Americans assume from their physical appearance that they must be foreigners. Representative Norman Y. Mineta of California, a Japanese American, wryly recalled the compliment paid to him by an American corporation executive: "My, Mr. Congressman, you speak good English."

Similarly, many Americans automatically consider Asian Americans to be linked to their ancestral lands. When the Communists suppressed dissident Chinese students in Beijing in 1989, American reporters interviewed Chinese Americans for their opinions—as if their skin pigmentation endowed them with inside information. Japanese Americans are often blamed for Japan's economic policies. In a California town not long ago, the walls of a Japanese American community center were smeared with slogans like "Nip, Go Back to Asia." More recently, a white man in Los Angeles spurned a Japanese American Girl Scout selling cookies, saying, "I only buy from American girls." Sensitive to such incidents, Robert T. Matsui, a California congressman of Japanese descent, told the *Los Angeles Times*, "I'm aware that my free trade position could be interpreted as 'he's with Japan.' It annoys me that I have to be a little more careful."

Asian Americans hold the highest percentage of managerial posts of any group in the country, and the scientists and engineers among them are coveted by companies throughout the nation. But outside of firms they have founded themselves, most run into a familiar glass ceiling as they seek to climb into board rooms they see from below. A study of the top executives of the Fortune 500 discovered that only 0.3 percent had Asian surnames. The *New York Times* reported in January 1992 that while Asian Americans comprised 26 percent of the engineers and 12 percent of the managers at the Hewlett Packard plant in Silicon Valley, there was not a single senior executive among them. Or as Jim Tso, a spokesman for the Organization of Chinese Americans, has put it: "In the past, we had the coolie who slaved. Today we have the high-tech coolie."

Many American companies maintain that Asian Americans, despite their technical talents, lack leadership ability. A particular criticism of recent immigrants is that their flawed English prevents them from communicating with other employees. Their reluctance to socialize with fellow workers, which may reflect their uneasiness in a new environment, is also viewed as incompatible with American corporate culture. But these observations, if sometimes valid, are often pretexts for racism, as mirrored in the numbers of discrimination cases won by Asian Americans in federal and state courts.

In many instances, Asian Americans go into business for themselves out of frustration. David Lam, who was born in China and earned a Ph.D. at the Massachusetts Institute of Technology, resigned from Hewlett Packard after a white American protégé was promoted over him, and founded his own Silicon Valley software company, Expert Edge, which is now a multimillion dollar operation. His and other such firms, shunned by American banks, have had to raise capital in Hong Kong or Taiwan, a practice that taints them as "aliens." Numbers of Asian Americans have left their professions for fields where they feel less stigmatized by race. Yun Pang, a Korean American with a graduate business degree, quit a New York insurance company to open a retail store after seeing an Asian American colleague bypassed by white Americans. As he remarked, "I thought, 'this guy is good, but if he's not making it, neither will I'."

Asian newcomers with special skills, hoping for careers in America, frequently learn to their distress that their professional credentials are discounted, and their only alternative is to accept humbler jobs. This is particularly true in medicine. Some 20 percent of the doctors in the United States were trained abroad, and nearly three-quarters of these are aliens.

The Asians among them came largely from India and the Philippines during the 1960s, when they were granted preferential admission to ease the scarcity of physicians in America. The shortage later became a surplus, and immigrant physicians now face stiffer certification examinations than do the graduates of U.S. medical schools—despite evidence that they are equally competent. A further complication is posed by different licensing requirements in different states, and numbers of doctors of Asian origin, unable to practice, go into research or even quit the field. Since they are best suited to treat Asian newcomers whose language and culture they know, barring them from practice penalizes immigrant communities most in need of health care.

At the bottom of the scale, many Asians are neglected by public agencies responsible for their defense against predatory employers. This situation is endemic in Chinatowns populated by newcomers engaged in menial tasks. Though many have skills, they are trapped by their inability to speak English, and they lack the time and energy to learn. They serve around the clock in restaurants as waiters and dishwashers. Chinese garment workers, most of them employed by Chinese entrepreneurs, are often confined to sweatshops located in lofts without fire escapes or in cellars without exits. They labor long hours, frequently at less than the minimum wage, and to make ends meet they take work home, a violation of the law. Many are teenagers. They have no medical or unemployment insurance. Their bosses, whose businesses are shaky, often withhold their salaries, and they rarely protest for fear of being dismissed. Many have been smuggled into America from China by criminal rings that indenture them until they repay their passage, which can run to thousands of dollars; default may cost them their lives. As undocumented aliens they cannot object to the authorities without risking deportation.

Many Asian Americans also allege discrimination at universities. The lament sounds paradoxical, given the fact that proportionally more are enrolled in colleges than any other group in the country. Their representation, moreover, has soared in such elite institutions as Harvard, Yale and the University of California at Berkeley. Still, they complain that they are subjected to unstated quotas that favor athletes, the children of alumni and applicants from selected geographical areas. They also argue that their high test scores, which ought to make them ideal candidates, work against them. College officials reject such charges, but in 1990 a federal probe found that the University of California at Los Angeles had discriminated against Asian American graduate students. Though criticism of affirmative action is taboo on campuses, numbers of Asian Americans privately deplore quotas that admit blacks and Hispanics less qualified than themselves.

Though racial crime is chiefly aimed at blacks, Asian Americans have not been spared crimes of this kind. In 1987 white youths calling themselves "dotbusters" killed two Indian Americans in New Jersey. Vietnamese fishermen in Texas and Florida have been attacked by white rivals. In July 1989 a Chinese immigrant was slain in North Carolina by two white brothers who claimed to be avenging the death of a brother in Vietnam. One was sentenced to 37 and the other to 4 years in prison. The incident reflected the extent to which some white Americans cannot distinguish one Asian from another—a tendency illustrated most vividly in the Vincent Chin case, which to many Asian Americans epitomizes the threat of racial violence that confronts them all.

On the night of June 19, 1982, Chin, a Chinese American engineering student, went with friends to a suburban Detroit go-go bar. There he got into a brawl with Ronald Ebens, a jobless automobile worker, who mistook him for a Japanese and, reportedly making racial remarks, blamed him for the industry's plight. Ebens and his stepson, Michael Nitz, later spotted Chin outside a nearby restaurant, where they clubbed him to death with a baseball bat. County judge Charles Kaufman allowed them to plead guilty to manslaughter rather than face a homicide charge, placed them on probation for three years and fined them $3,750 each.

The ruling sparked an outcry from Asian American and other groups, whose protests carried the case to a federal court, where Ebens and Nitz were charged with depriving Chin of his civil rights. Nitz was acquitted and Ebens, found guilty, was sentenced to 25 years in jail. Ebens's conviction was later reversed because of a judicial error, and he was acquitted in a retrial in May 1987. In a civil settlement, he agreed to pay the Chin estate $1.5 million over time, but he has been out of work and broke for years.

If Chin was a casualty of mistaken identity, he may have also been the inadvertent victim of hatred misdirected against Japanese Americans because of Japan's economic success in the United States. The hostility is especially visible in Detroit, where some United Automobile Worker locals have distributed anti-Japanese posters and bumper stickers. Racism has been fueled by Michigan politicians like Democratic Representative John

D. Dingell, who has talked of Americans losing jobs to "little yellow men." Surveys show, however, that most Americans not only continue to buy Japanese products but blame America's leaders for the nation's economic failings.

Racial tensions have been particularly intense between black Americans and Korean immigrants. In 1990 a conflict roiled Brooklyn as blacks boycotted a Korean grocer alleged to have assaulted a black woman and assaulted three young Vietnamese, whom they mistook for Koreans. Blacks killed seven Koreans in Los Angeles in 1991, but the violence there has not been one-sided. In March a Korean woman shopkeeper killed a black girl after accusing her of stealing a bottle of orange juice. Convicted of voluntary manslaughter, the woman was sentenced to five years' probation—a ruling that outraged the city's black and other groups and prompted demands for the judge's recall. The black movie director Spike Lee touches on the tragic irony of racial minorities battling each other in his film, "Do The Right Thing," when a Korean grocer, fearful of rioting blacks, desperately shouts at them, "I not white! I black! Like you! Same!"

Korean and black leaders have tried to mediate these disputes, which largely reflect cultural differences. Many Korean immigrants, as they themselves concede, seem to be aloof because of their unfamiliarity with English—a trait often regarded by blacks as animosity. Numbers of blacks resent the success of newcomers in running small businesses in depressed neighborhoods where they themselves have failed. Many also believe that Koreans receive special bank loans when, in fact, they rely on their own credit unions. They may be spurred toward violence against Koreans by performers like rap star "Ice Cube," whose song "Black Korea" contains a lyric: "Pay respect to the black fist, or we'll burn your store right down to a crisp." The entertainer later apologized to Korean American leaders, saying somewhat cryptically that his song was "directed at a few stores where my friends and I have had actual problems." Some Koreans believe, however, that he contributed to the attacks against them in the Los Angeles riots of April 1992.

Equally ominous has been the rise of Asian criminal gangs, ranging from bands of young Vietnamese in California to highly organized Chinese syndicates that operate in New York, San Francisco and other cities. Though they prey chiefly on Asian immigrants, some are widening their field. At a hearing in 1991, Senator Sam Nunn of Georgia, head of a subcommittee probing Asian crime, called their activities "very frightening."

Scores of Vietnamese gangs maraud Little Saigon, an area south of Los Angeles populated largely by refugees. Armed with knives, pistols and even semiautomatic weapons, they rob stores and extort payments from merchants. They specialize in "home invasions," breaking into the houses of affluent Vietnamese to terrorize them into handing over valuables. The victims are reluctant to inform the police or testify in court out of fear that the suspects, often released on bail or recognizance, will retaliate against them. Nor does the prospect of jail frighten offenders who have risked their lives to flee Vietnam and spent years in refugee camps.

But according to William S. Sessions, director of the Federal Bureau of Investigation, the "most serious threat" comes from Chinese criminal organizations. Some are linked to triads, traditional secret societies, based in Hong Kong and Taiwan. Most business and fraternal associations known as "tongs" are legitimate, but several of their members are involved in illicit enterprises. An official investigation conducted in 1990 found that such groups extorted money from 81 percent of restaurants and 66 percent of other businesses in New York's Chinatown, where they manage illegal gambling, prostitution and other rackets. Through connections to drug rings in Southeast Asia, they account for an estimated 70 percent of the heroin traffic in New York. Though these activities are alarming, they should be seen in perspective. A few immigrants have always turned to crime as a shortcut to success, so that the small percentage of Asian American lawbreakers are essentially no different from Italians who joined the Mafia or Jews who founded Murder, Incorporated.

Recent decades have witnessed the expansion of advocacy groups dedicated to promoting equality and justice for Asian Americans. But though these groups have had a certain impact, Asian Americans will not exert real influence until they enter the political arena more dynamically than they have so far—and that, most would agree, is their next challenge.

8

Politics

"The day cannot be far when some district on the Pacific slope will contain a majority of Chinese voters, and will elect a Chinaman to Congress," the *California Alta* forecast in August 1868. But nearly a century passed before Asian Americans began to enter politics, and even now they are conspicuously absent from elected office. Only five sit in Congress. While they comprise 10 percent of California's population, not one belongs to the state legislature. Nor do they play a major political role in cities like New York and San Francisco, where their numbers are substantial. Commenting on the phenomenon recently, Michael Woo, the grandson of a Chinese immigrant and the only Asian American on the Los Angeles City Council, called it a "disgrace."

Asian Americans hold appointed positions at every level of government, and they are active in advocacy movements. As a group they have been effective in such efforts as the campaign to win redress for the Japanese Americans interned during World War II and the drive to retry Vincent Chin's murderers. Their support has also been vital to mainstream American candidates. So they clearly have the potential to compete for office. But, for various reasons, the majority flinch from direct participation in politics.

Apart from Japanese Americans, most Asian Americans are immigrants. Many though not all come from countries with despotic and corrupt regimes, and are either unacquainted with the democratic process or distrust government. Many are riveted more on news from their homelands than on events in America. As newcomers they are usually too busy making a living and educating their children to focus on politics. Though many are not yet naturalized, even the citizens among them seldom vote.

They are almost evenly divided between Republicans and Democrats, a mirror of their diversity. But a large proportion are independents, which can exclude them from casting ballots in primary contests. Their lack of party affiliation further hinders them from acting collectively.

There is also a cultural element in their aversion to politics. Asians have traditionally set the welfare of their families as their top priority. Moreover, they view politics as less rewarding than business and less prestigious than science. Art Wang, a Chinese American lawyer and member of the Washington state legislature, has recalled: "My mother sees me not as a politician but as an attorney, a profession that in her eyes has a higher status."

Their diversity also discourages Asian Americans from forging political coalitions, as many other ethnic and racial groups do. In a local Los Angeles election not long ago, Japanese, Korean and Filipino American candidates ran against each other, thereby assuring the victory of a white contender. In addition, the rough and tumble game of politics tends to repel Asian Americans, and they prefer not to get involved. As Judy Chu, a Chinese American and former mayor of Monterey Park, California, a heavily Asian community, has explained: "Taking a lot of risks and a lot of criticism, asserting a point of view and talking about yourself— that is not in the Asian nature."

Nor can the history of Asians in America be forgotten. Institutionally denied their civil rights for generations, they were slow to engage in politics.

As they poured into the United States during the late 19th and early 20th centuries, newcomers from Europe rapidly learned that political power was the path to equality and justice. The Irish, among the first to grasp that reality, built political machines in Boston and New York, thereby inspiring Jewish, Italian and other immigrants to seek public office or to lobby for their rights. Their struggle was arduous. As late as 1930, President Herbert Hoover reacted against jibes from Fiorello LaGuardia, the Italian- born mayor of New York, by saying, "Go back to where you belong.... Like a lot of other foreign spawn you do not appreciate the country that supports and tolerates you."

Though most early Chinese newcomers hoped to return to China, many sought acceptance as full-fledged Americans. In 1852 a group of Chinese merchants addressed an appeal to the San Francisco authorities: "If the privileges of your laws are open to us, some of us will undoubtedly acquire your habits, your language, your ideas, your feelings, your morals, your forms and become citizens of your country." Such pleas were rejected, however. Even after the Civil War, when freed black slaves were accorded citizenship, Congress refused Chinese the same right. In 1870, arguing on their behalf, Senator Charles Sumner of Massachusetts maintained that the Constitution makes "no distinction of color." But not until 1943 could Chinese immigrants apply for naturalization—and it took nine more years before racial barriers to citizenship were lifted for other Asians.

As citizens they would have certainly supported one or another of the political parties, as other minorities did in an effort to improve their status. As it was, they were ignored by American politicians, who either saw no benefit in wooing disenfranchised aliens or placated bigots whose votes counted. But the Chinese formed organizations that were the precursors of advocacy groups that have since fought with notable success for the Asian American cause.

The first, created in 1854 in San Francisco, was the Chinese Consolidated Benevolent Association, which served as an intermediary between City Hall and Chinatown. Branches spread around the country, where they fulfilled a similar function. As discriminatory laws and ordinances against Chinese spread, they enlisted American attorneys who managed to have many of the onerous statutes voided in state and federal courts.

But its rotating chairmanship, a device contrived to share power among its diverse members, made the association unwieldy. It was often split as well by factional disputes that reflected clan rivalries. Headed by Cantonese, it also failed later to accommodate to immigrants from other regions of China. Nevertheless, it has remained the voice of the old Chinatown establishment—though its authority has been challenged by other groups.

In 1895, reacting against a white supremacist movement calling itself the Native Sons of the Golden West, a group of American-born Chinese in California founded the Native Sons of the Golden State. A decade later, when the Supreme Court finally ruled that Chinese born in the United States were citizens, they renamed it the Chinese American Citizens Alliance—a sign that they intended to demand their rights. Directed from San Francisco, chapters in other cities fought against discrimination and urged Chinese Americans to engage in politics. In 1935, the organization began publishing *The Chinese Digest*, the country's first English-language Chinese American newspaper.

As the number of Chinese American citizens grew after World War I, so did their commitment to politics. Many campaigned for President Franklin D. Roosevelt's reelection in 1936, and some were themselves elected to local office in California and Hawaii. By the 1950s, partly to display its anti-Communist zeal following Mao Zedong's rise to power in China, the Chinese American Citizens Alliance had shifted toward support of the Republicans, and its opponents formed a Chinese American Democratic Club. So, despite their divisions, Chinese Americans were at last exercising the rights they should have been given nearly a century before. But they trailed Japanese Americans in the creation of a countrywide political organization.

Having brought few women with them—and barred by laws from intermarriage—most Chinese in America before World War II were bachelors. But early Japanese newcomers, allowed to import wives, bore children who were citizens by virtue of birth, which enabled them to enter politics more rapidly than the Chinese had.

During the 1920s, as they came of age, numbers of Nisei doctors, lawyers and other professionals regarded themselves as Americans first. They enrolled in the Democratic and Republican parties, and founded patriotic groups like the American Loyalty League. In 1930 delegates from several of these groups formed the Japanese American Citizens League, to this day the community's most important organization.

Its leaders were sensitive to discrimination, but they stressed that success combined with total allegiance to the United States would overcome prejudice. Equaling Americans was not enough, proclaimed one of their spokesmen: "We must *surpass* them—by developing our powers to the point of genius if necessary." A few years later they pledged to defend America "against all enemies, foreign and domestic . . . without any reservations whatsoever."

Faithful to that vow, they raised few objections to the internment of Japanese Americans following Japan's attack on Pearl Harbor, and some even cooperated in facilitating the move. There was probably little else they could have done then, yet the move left them vulnerable to criticism from those who resisted internment and from younger Japanese Americans after World War II. But, under new leaders, the Japanese American Citizens League was later instrumental in the campaign to indemnify the internees.

Many Asians in America were meanwhile concerned chiefly with politics in their native lands. Early Korean newcomers agitated for Korea's independence from Japan. Asian Indians in California at the turn of the century conspired against British colonial rule of India, but their movement collapsed during World War I, when they were accused of colluding with German agents. Sun Yat Sen, founder of the Chinese Republic in 1911, received substantial funds from Chinese Americans. During the 1930s, preoccupied by China's resistance to Japanese aggression, Chinese Americans overwhelmingly backed Generalissimo Chiang Kai-shek's Nationalists. Chinatowns became pro-Nationalist bastions, and they ardently opposed the Communists after their conquest of China in 1949. Some Chinese Americans even cooperated with the "China Lobby," whose right-wing American militants used the "loss" of China as a pretext to smear their liberal rivals. They may have adopted that stance for protective reasons, since any hint of sympathy for the Communists would have exposed them to the "Red hunters" of the period. By the 1960s, however, they were being defied by radical young Chinese Americans inspired by Mao Zedong's doctrines, who sought to bring down the old Chinatown elite. The excesses of Mao's Cultural Revolution, exacerbated by the Communist suppression of dissident students in Beijing in June 1989, estranged most Chinese Americans from China. But it also prompted in many the feeling that, while they were Americans, they had to assert their Chinese origins. After the events in Beijing in 1989, for example, the celebrated architect I. M. Pei and other prominent Chinese Americans organized the Committee of 100 in hopes of influencing U.S. policy toward China.

The Philippine presidential election of 1986 similarly aroused the Filipino American partisans of Ferdinand Marcos and Corazon Aquino. Korea's future captures the attention of Korean Americans, and Taiwanese Americans have lobbied for years for Taiwan's independence. Japanese Americans, the most acculturated of Asian Americans, closely monitor relations between the United States and Japan, partly out of fear that friction may spur racial sentiment against them—as has indeed occurred in the aftermath of President Bush's ill-fated journey to Tokyo in January 1992.

Many Indochinese refugees, profoundly attached to their native soil, dream of returning home. Young Cambodians have gone back to Cambodia to rebuild their benighted nation. Older Vietnamese constantly discuss developments in Vietnam, and a few years ago some organized a commando squad in a futile attempt to oust the Communist regime. Accordingly, they tend to ignore the problems that face their communities in America. In Orange County, California, where more than 100,000 Vietnamese have settled, not a single one sits on a town council.

Asian Americans have not been alone in their concern with "homeland" issues. Cuban, Greek, Armenian, Italian, Irish and Polish Americans have long tracked events in the "old country," and the vast majority of Jewish Americans are committed to the security of Israel.

Not until 1956 did the first Asian American vault into national politics. Given the scarcity of Asian Indians then in America, he was an oddity—a Sikh from the Punjab. Dalip Singh Saund had come to California 26 years earlier and thrived in farming before predominantly white voters sent him to the House of Representatives, where he served three terms. But the political breakthrough for Asian Americans was Hawaii's admission to the Union in 1959, which brought to the U.S. Senate such figures as Hiram Fong, a Chinese American millionaire, and later Daniel Inouye, a Japanese American war hero, as well as bringing several new members to the House of Representatives. California subsequently elected other Asian Americans, like Senator Samuel I. Hayakawa, a prominent and somewhat eccentric professor of linguistics. Democrat or Republican, they have not acted as representatives of their racial group.

Even though they are concentrated on the West and East coasts, Asian Americans are too dispersed and diverse to form a solid bloc. Moreover, many of them do not vote. In California, fewer than 300,000 of the state's nearly 3 million Asian Americans are registered voters—a rate far behind that of whites, blacks and Hispanics. During the 1990 elections in San Francisco, a city with more than 200,000 Asian Americans, only about 17,000 voted. The same picture emerged in Flushing, New York, where a new district was created to accommodate its 50,000 Asian Americans, who account for 31 percent of the population. Despite the fact that a Chinese American candidate was in the race for City Council in 1991, only 6.7 percent of Asian Americans registered to vote—and fewer than 500 of them were of Chinese descent. As the *New York Times* commented, "Demographics alone cannot win an election."

Thus the success of Asian American politicians hinges on a reaching out to a broad spectrum of voters. Robert Matsui and Norman Mineta, both of Japanese origin and the only Asian American congressmen from mainland America, represent districts with only a small minority of Asian

Americans. Of California's 40 Asian American mayors and city council members, all except two were elected by voters belonging to groups other than their own. One of the exceptions was in Monterey Park, the only town in the United States whose population is mostly Asian American.

Still, their communities can serve as a base for Asian American politicians. Such was the experience of Art Wang, whose Tacoma district is less than 2 percent Asian American. While counting on Asian American volunteers at the start to ring doorbells and raise funds, he realized that he had to widen his appeal to white, black and other voters, and he focused on issues that struck a chord with them. "You can't paint yourself into an ethnic corner," he has noted. "You run as a politician who happens to be an Asian American, not as an Asian American politician."

Asian American voters often support white mainstream politicians, perhaps in the belief that they are have more clout than Asian Americans. Nancy Pelosi, an American of Italian origin, is regularly returned to Congress from a California district with the largest number of Asian Americans outside Hawaii. In the recent San Francisco mayoralty race, most of Chinatown favored Frank Jordan, a former police chief, over Tom Hsieh, his Chinese American rival. Representative Stephen Solarz of New York, chair of the House Subcommittee on Asian Affairs, receives large donations from Asian American groups. During the 1988 presidential campaign, Asian Americans gave more than $1 million each to George Bush and Michael Dukakis—making them second only to Jewish Americans as contributors. Bush won about 61 percent of the Asian American vote, according to Tony Chen of the Republican National Committee. However, Asian Americans hesitate to demand favors in exchange for their donations, maybe out of their unfamiliarity with the traditional "spoils system."

While it is difficult to discern a consensus among Asian Americans, support for the Republicans appears to be growing. The trend partly mirrors the conservatism of many Japanese, Chinese and Indian American entrepreneurs who believe, like other American businesspeople, that Republicans best represent their interests. The Republicans also seem to have the edge among Indochinese and Korean Americans, who fiercely oppose communism in their ancestral lands and feel that the party shares their view. Two ultraconservative congressmen, Dana Rohrabacher and Robert K. Dornan, come from districts in southern California, an area heavily populated by Americans of Indochinese and Korean descent. Asian

Americans concerned with social issues, chiefly in cities, lean toward the Democrats. But many are recent immigrants who cannot vote.

Bush has named a record number of Asian Americans to federal jobs. Among them are Elaine Chao, the Peace Corps director, Julia Chang Bloch, the ambassador to Nepal, and Ming Chen Hsu of the Federal Maritime Commission. But Bloch has noted that qualified Asian Americans are almost invisible in the top echelons of the administration. "It is obvious," she recently said, "that education and academic excellence do not automatically produce professional success."

The accomplishments of their advocacy organizations testify to the political dynamism and proficiency of Asian Americans. They cannot truly promote their interests, however, until they run for public office or acquire the leverage to influence elections by forming more effective pressure groups. As Robert Matsui has remarked, they "have not developed the level of sophistication necessary to advance in the political system." But given their diversity and small numbers, the prospects for their making an impact are slim unless they can cement coalitions among themselves and with other groups while increasing their voter turnout. They have been learning that lesson over the past decade. So, just as they are making strides in other fields, they are likely to move sooner or later from the sidelines into the nation's main political arenas.

Further Readings on Asian Americans

General:

Daniels, Roger. *Asian America: Chinese and Japanese in the United States since 1850* (Seattle: University of Washington Press, 1988).

Kitano, Harry H. L., and Roger Daniels. *Asian Americans: Emerging Minorities* (Englewood Cliffs, NJ: Prentice-Hall, 1988).

Gardner, Robert W., Bryant Robey, and Peter C. Smith. "Asian Americans: Growth, Change and Diversity," *Population Bulletin*, Vol. 40, no. 4 (February 1989).

Takaki, Ronald. *Strangers From a Different Shore: A History of Asian Americans* (Boston: Little Brown, 1989).

U.S. Commission on Civil Rights. *Civil Rights Issues Facing Asian Americans in the 1990s* (Washington, D.C.: February 1992).

Chinese Americans:

Chan, Sucheng, ed. *Entry Denied: Exclusion and the Chinese Community in America, 1882–1943* (Philadelphia: Temple University Press, 1991).

Chinn, Thomas W., ed. *A History of the Chinese in California: A Syllabus* (San Francisco: Chinese Historical Society of America, 1969).

Fessler, Loren W. *Chinese in America: Stereotyped Past, Changing Present* (New York: Vantage, 1983).

Isaacs, Harold R. *Scratches on Our Minds: American Views of China and India* (New York: M. E. Sharpe, 1980).

Kwong, Peter. *Chinatown, New York: Labor and Politics, 1930–1950* (New York: Monthly Review, 1981).

——————. *The New Chinatown* (New York: Hill and Wang, 1987).

Nee, Victor G., and Brett de Bary. *Longtime Californ': A Documentary Study of an American Chinatown* (New York: Pantheon, 1973).

Pan, Lynn. *Sons of the Yellow Emperor: A History of the Chinese Diaspora* (Boston: Little, Brown, 1990).

Sung, Betty Lee. *The Story of the Chinese in America* (New York: Collier, 1967).

Tsai, Shih-shan Henry. *The Chinese Experience in America* (Bloomington: Indiana University Press, 1986).

Yu, Connie Young. *Chinatown, San Jose, USA* (San Jose, CA: San Jose Historical Museum Association, 1991).

Japanese Americans:

Daniels, Roger. *The Politics of Prejudice: The Anti-Japanese Movement in California and the Struggle for Japanese Exclusion* (Berkeley: University of California Press, 1962).

Hisashi, Tsurutani. *America-Bound: The Japanese and the Opening of the American West* (Tokyo: Japan Times, 1977).

Hohri, William M. *Repairing American: An Account of the Movement for Japanese-American Redress* (Pullman: Washington State University Press, 1988).

Ichioka, Yuji. *The Issei: The World of the First Generation Japanese American Immigrants, 1885–1924* (New York: Free Press, 1988).

Irons, Peter. *Justice at War: The Story of the Japanese American Internment Cases* (New York: Oxford University Press, 1983).

Johnson, Sheila K. *The Japanese Through American Eyes* (Stanford: Stanford University Press, 1988).

Kitano, Harry H. L. *Japanese Americans: The Evolution of a Subculture* (Englewood Cliffs, NJ: Prentice-Hall, 1969).

Mura, David. *Turning Japanese: Memoirs of a Sansei* (New York: Atlantic Monthly, 1990).

O'Brien, David J., and Stephen S. Fugita. *The Japanese American Experience* (Bloomington: Indiana University Press, 1991).

Tateishi, John. *And Justice for All: An Oral History of the Japanese American Detention Camps* (New York: Random House, 1984).

Weglyn, Michi. *Years of Infamy: The Untold Story of America's Concentration Camps* (New York: Morrow, 1976).

Filipino Americans:

Bulosan, Carlos. *America is in the Heart: A Personal History* (Seattle: University of Washington Press, 1973).

Cordova, Fred. *Filipinos: Forgotten Asian Americans* (Dubuque: Kendall/Hunt, 1983).

Kim, Hyung-chan, and Cynthia C. Meija, eds. *The Filipinos in America 1898–1974: A Chronology and Fact Book* (Dobbs Ferry, NY: Oceana, 1976).

Korean Americans:

Hyun, Peter. *Man Sei! The Making of an Korean American* (Honolulu: University of Hawaii Press, 1986).

Kim, Hyuing–chan, ed. *The Korean Diaspora: Historical and Sociological Studies of Korean Immigration* (Santa Barbara, CA: ABC-CLIO, 1977).

Lee, Mark Paik. *Quiet Odyssey: A Pioneer Korean Woman in America* (Seattle: University of Washington Press, 1990).

Light, Ivan, and Edna Bonacich. *Immigrant Entrepreneurs: Koreans in Los Angeles, 1965–1982* (Berkeley: University of California Press, 1988).

Yu, Diana. *Winds of Change: Korean Women in America* (Silver Spring, MD: Women's Institute Press, 1991).

Indian Americans:

Chandrasekhar, S., ed. *From India to America: A Brief History of Immigration* (La Jolla, CA: Population Review Publications, 1982).

Coelho, George V. *Changing Images of America: A Study of Indian Students' Perceptions* (Glencoe, IL: Free Press, 1958).

Daniels, Roger. *History of Indian Immigration to the United States: An Interpretive Essay* (New York: The Asia Society, 1989).

Saran, Parmatma. *The Asian Indian Experience in the United States* (Cambridge, MA: Schenkman, 1985).

Indochinese Americans:

Ashabranner, Brent, and Melissa Ashabranner. *Into a Strange Land: Unaccompanied Refugee Youth in America* (New York: Putnam, 1987).

Caplan, Nathan, John K. Whitmore, and Marcella H. Choy. *The Boat People and Achievement in America* (Ann Arbor: University of Michigan Press, 1989).

Freeman, James M. *Hearts of Sorrow: Vietnamese–American Lives* (Stanford, CA: Stanford University Press, 1989).

Morgan, Scott M., and Elizabeth Colson, eds. *People in Upheaval* (New York: Center for Migration Studies, 1987).

About the Authors

Stanley Karnow's most recent book, *In Our Image: America's Empire in the Philippines*, won the Pulitzer Prize in History in 1990. His other books include *Mao and China: From Revolution to Revolution* and *Vietnam: A History*. He is now writing a book on the Asian experience in America. He was a correspondent in Asia for *Time* and later for the *Washington Post*. A graduate of Harvard, he returned there as a Nieman Fellow and was subsequently a Fellow at both the John F. Kennedy School of Government and the East Asia Research Center.

Nancy Yoshihara is an editorial writer at the *Los Angeles Times*. Before joining the editorial board she was a staff writer for the business section, covering the Pacific Rim, retailing and marketing. She was part of a team of reporters that in 1989 put together the award-winning series "Working for the Japanese." Earlier she was a Jefferson Fellow at the East-West Center in Honolulu. A graduate of the University of California at Los Angeles, she also earned a master's degree in journalism there.

Donors to The Asia Society Project on Asian Americans

Freedom Forum

Dole Food Company, Inc.

ARCO Foundation

AT&T Foundation

The James Irvine Foundation

Rockefeller Foundation

Toyota Motor Sales U.S.A.

CITIBANK

Pacific Bell

Anheuser-Busch Companies

Mikasa/Kenwood, Inc.

Andrew B. Kim

Southern California Edison Company

United Airlines